D0432610

MANY OF OUR CUSTOMERS
HAVE BEEN COMING TO US FOR CENTURIES

SOME FOR CONSIDERABLY LONGER

www.monstersupplies.org

FROM OUR
EVERYDAY NECESSITIES RANGE

HOXTON STREET
MONSTER SUPPPLIES'

FANG
FLOSS

— Made From Biodegradable 3 Ply Jute Twine —

Our marvellously strong Fang Floss is invaluable in cleaning where traditional sticks and brushes can't reach, removing all common forms of fang-matter, including: brains, gore, bones, viscera, entrails, seaweed, toffee and much more.

Ideal for the 21st-century monster who believes chomping through flesh and bone shouldn't have to put a crimp on post-mauling socializing.

If your grocer does not keep it in stock, ask him to order it for you.

For Igor

---

*A Disgustingly
Discerning
Founder
and
Monster Assistant
Extraordinaire*

THE

HOXTON STREET MONSTER SUPPLIES COOKBOOK

EVERYDAY RECIPES FOR THE LIVING, DEAD AND UNDEAD

MITCHELL
BEAZLEY

— Revised edition featuring recipes suitable for humans —

CONTENTS

INTRODUCTION

Three thousand years ago, a dinner invite from a Troll or a Cyclops would have been unheard of. Monster communities were physically spread out and many lived a hand-to-mouth existence, hunting animals on the plains and occasionally venturing into settlements to prey on humans. The only nod towards culinary expertise was the fire pit— essentially a means of warmth but also used to cook tougher cuts of meat.

Luckily, times have changed—transport links, monster markets, refrigeration (for maintaining the optimum level of decay) and a bounty of health and cookery literature have resulted in monsters elevating food from its lowly status of survival fodder to something that is eagerly anticipated and enjoyed. Menus are now planned in advance, ingredients are carefully chosen and friends and family gather together to enjoy meals socially.

PROVENANCE

Monsters have become savvier with regard to where ingredients are sourced and produced. A surge in the popularity of organic human dismemberers, free-range farms and ethically sourced body parts led to the closure of many factory farms in the last century, with suppliers forced to disclose the provenance of every last toenail and brain. There has also been a rise in the number of homotarians—Swamp Creatures and more enlightened Vampires, in particular, are choosing to embrace a human-meat-free lifestyle and form bonds of friendship with humans rather than serving them up for dinner.

ALLERGIES AND DIETARY REQUIREMENTS

As well as ensuring the quality of ingredients, many home cooks also have to contend with the increase in allergies and food intolerances, particularly among monster offspring. It is believed this is largely due to a generation of fast-food humans entering the food chain (specimens with fat-clogged arteries are now strictly prohibited for monster consumption and can only be sold as minions).

In the meantime, allergy sufferers need to steer clear of certain ingredients that could cause a reaction. Common conditions include: hair fever, pus intolerance, human-dander allergy, blood boils and eyeball dermatitis. It is advised to always check the labels of pre-packaged body parts; if in doubt, buy a whole carcass from a reputable retailer and ask your local dismemberer to break it down for you.

USING THE BOOK

As more monsters indulge their passion for cuisine, they are increasingly looking for recipe ideas for home cooking and entertaining. This collection of sweet and savoury dishes has taken traditional community favourites and updated them for the modern gourmand. With ingredients such as winter-flu pus, organic swamp water, Neanderthal guts and fairy brains now very difficult—or impossible—to source, centuries-old family favourites have dropped off the dinner menu. This revised edition of the cookbook is also suitable for humans looking to expand on their recipe repertoire.

The modern monster has a poor work-life balance—Zombies take twice as long to perform any task; Vampires work long night shifts; Swamp Creatures have very long commutes; and Giant Apes are dealing with deforestation. Everyone is looking for quick-fix snacks with accessible ingredients and, whether you're gut intolerant, human-friendly or follow a gluten-free or bone-restricted diet, you'll find plenty of inspiration in this book.

From party classics such as Strawberry Shortdeads (see page 52) to lunchtime liveners like Classic Orphan Marmalade (see page 97), you'll soon be wooing Werewolves, tempting Trolls, delighting Dragons and introducing Vampires to a whole host of bloodless midnight snacks.

ABOUT THE SHOP

If you happen to be strolling around the streets of East London, you might chance upon this splendidly appointed yet delightfully unassuming shopfront. Monsters have been crossing the threshold of Hoxton Street Monster Supplies since the shop opened back in 1818, with the local human population largely oblivious to the nocturnal comings and goings of the capital's Vampires, Zombies, Dragons, Sasquatches and Trolls.

Behind the traditional façade lies a wealth of everyday items for the living, dead and undead. As the only purveyor of monster supplies in London (and possibly in the world), we're proud of our long history of helping the monster community thrive in the heart of the city. From sweet treats like Cubed Earwax, to gifts like Bah! Humbugs, and Banshee Balls, this one-stop monster supply shop caters to every taste, whim and fancy.

One of our primary aims is to help our clientele navigate through the increasingly tricky terrain of the modern world, and to ensure that their traditional way of life isn't threatened and their culture is respected and protected. Our range of carefully crafted products, including Tinned Fear and Salt Made From Tears, enables customers to continue scaring, hunting, shape shifting, transmogrifying and reanimating with impunity.

THE HISTORY OF THE SHOP

Though the history of our shop is distinctly murky, we are fairly confident that Hoxton Street Monster Supplies was founded by Igor, the celebrated personal assistant to both Victor Frankenstein and Count Dracula. He subsequently worked closely with several other notable monsters, but after a tragic incident with a vat of snot found himself out of work. He fled Transylvania, and arrived in London in 1817.

His previous career meant Igor was a fount of knowledge when it came to remedies, personal grooming and fine consumables. He soon became a major player on the London monster social scene, with monsters travelling far and wide to ask him to procure hard-to-find remedies and groceries. Igor spotted a gap in the market and opened the shop on Hoxton Street. It quickly became a convening point for London's monster community—providing much-needed social contact, insider information on good scaring locations and, naturally, the finest range of gourmet monster groceries in the capital.

Fast-forward to 2010 when we completely overhauled and modernized the interior. Hundreds of years of cobwebs were cleared, electricity was installed and we even set up a website. Perhaps most controversially, the shop became fully visible and accessible to human customers.

Naturally, many of the older generation of monster clientele were alarmed by these sudden and dramatic changes. But they quickly appreciated not having to wear reading glasses when browsing the shelves, and being able to shop online during inclement weather.

THE CURSE OF CREATIVITY

Due to a rather inconvenient curse, all our profits go to the Ministry of Stories, a creative writing and mentoring charity for young humans. We are doing everything in our power to rectify this intolerable situation.

Golden Rules for Entertaining

Whether it's a family gathering or a dinner party for friends, the diverse dietary, social and cultural requirements of different members of the community mean that careful planning must take place before any event. From sending out invitations (large print for Cyclopses; simplified text for Zombies; voicemail for illiterate Giant Apes and Swamp Creatures), to choosing the menu and entertainment, social gatherings can be a balancing act of epic proportions. So, while it is perfectly possible to host a party with an eclectic guest list, it is advisable to follow a few simple guidelines for a successful celebration.

☞ If Vampires are on the guest list, be sure to start proceedings after dark and keep garlic *firmly off* the ingredients list—if possible, out of the house completely. You might also want to advise any human guests to wear a scarf or roll-neck jumper: Vampires can be very restrained in social situations but you don't want to risk temptation after a couple of aperitifs.

☞ If your party falls during a full moon, adjust the catering accordingly: Werewolves have *particularly voracious* appetites at this time and can devour twice the regular portion size of each course.

☞ Zombies take things *very slowly* so allow extra time for dinner and niceties. It is also advised to plan a simple menu around these guests—they're not the sharpest tools in the box and anything too complicated could quickly use up the few remaining brain cells they possess.

☞ *Under no circumstances* should you seat a Cyclops next to a Giant Spider. Despite their size, Cyclopses tend to be sensitive about their solitary eye and they might construe the seating plan as an underhand insult.

☞ If you have small humans, think carefully before inviting Under-the-Bed or In-the-Cupboard Monsters to your soirée. Although they rarely mix work with pleasure, they can *sometimes* mistake the suggestion of after-dinner party games as an open invitation to scare children witless in the name of light entertainment.

☞ Keep Swamp Creatures off the guest list if you've recently had new carpets fitted. Some hosts offer slime-proof onesies on arrival but there will inevitably be a certain amount of *leakage* during the course of the evening.

☞ Dragons and Yetis should be seated at *opposite ends* of the table for obvious reasons of temperature control—a hot Yeti does not make for a convivial dinner guest. If they do get a little flushed, open the freezer door and perch them in front of it for half an hour.

☞ Zombies are *very self-conscious* about shedding errant limbs and will often turn down dinner invitations for fear of dropping a finger into a fondue or losing a leg during a game of Twister. You can pre-empt this by supplying a large box or bag for life, in which they can deposit loose limbs and collect them when they leave.

Hoxton Street Monster Supplies

ESTᴰ 1818

~ Purveyor of Quality Goods for Monsters of Every Kind ~

SWEETS
&
PASTILLES

INCLUDING
CRUNCHING BONE TOFFEE
& FAIRY BRAIN FUDGE

CRUNCHING BONE TOFFEE

In days gone by, Bone Toffee was a particular favourite of Werewolves and Giants, as the mouth-watering combination of lightly crushed human bones and sweet toffee was a rare treat. If you're a stickler for the classics and can source human bones, you can ask your local human dismemberer to crunch them for you. If not, we're confident you'll find our 21st-century version of the recipe most agreeable.

Sufficient.—for 175g (6oz) of toffee

about 50g (2oz) milk chocolate,
    broken into pieces
50g (2oz) firm toffees
4 tablespoons milk
1 tablespoon vegetable oil
75g (3oz) popcorn kernels

Method.—Melt the chocolate in a small heatproof bowl set over a small saucepan of gently simmering water.

Meanwhile, unwrap the toffees and put them in a polythene bag. Place on a chopping board and tap firmly with a rolling pin until the toffees have broken into small pieces. Tip the pieces into a small saucepan and add the milk. Cook over the lowest possible heat until the toffee has melted (this will take several minutes, depending on the firmness of the toffee). Remove from the heat.

Put the oil in a large saucepan with a tight-fitting lid and heat for 1 minute. Add the popcorn kernels and cover with the lid. Cook until the popping sound stops, then tip the corn out on to a large baking sheet or roasting tin and leave to cool for 5 minutes.

Using a teaspoon, drizzle lines of the toffee sauce over the corn until lightly coated. Drizzle with lines of the melted chocolate in the same way.

CRUNCHING BONE TOFFEE

Try if you can to source your humans from around gyms and exercise clubs.
Their strong, healthy bones provide a pleasant crunch.

BLOODSUCKER PASTILLES

The freshest human blood was traditionally used to achieve the soft, gooey consistency of these pastilles. They were commonly prepared for baby monsters during weaning, as they could use their gums to chew and gain an early bloodlust. This updated version is no less delicious—serve them as a sweet snack to elderly family members who no longer have the luxury of a full set of fangs.

Sufficient.—for about 25 pastilles

1 tablespoon vegetable oil or sunflower oil,
    plus extra for oiling
400 g (13 oz) strawberries, hulled
2 cm (¾ inch) thick slice of lemon, rind
    and any pips removed
450 g (14½ oz) jam sugar
30 g (1¼ oz) caster sugar

Method.—Line a 15 cm (6 inch) square dish with baking paper and grease with the oil. Blitz the strawberries and lemon slice in a food processor or blender, then press the mixture through a fine sieve into a stainless steel pan.

Add the jam sugar and mix well, then place over a medium heat and bring to the boil. When the mixture is bubbling vigorously, cook for 35 minutes, stirring occasionally, until thick and a little darker in colour. Pour carefully into the prepared dish and leave to cool for about 1 hour.

Lift out of the dish and peel off the paper, then cut the mixture into about 25 pastilles using a lightly oiled mini metal cookie cutter. Alternatively, lightly oil a large, sharp knife and cut into small squares. Spread the caster sugar on a plate, then roll each pastille in the sugar until coated, brushing away any excess.

AFTER-GORGING BREATH MINTS

These mints will help solve the age-old conundrum of rancid breath following a brain banquet, so keep a few close to hand at dinner parties and first dates. Nothing quite dampens the ardour of a Zombie suitor like human-organ halitosis: a quick suck on a breath mint will greatly improve your chances of some undead corporeal carousing.

Sufficient.—for about 100 mints

150 g (5 oz) icing sugar, sifted, plus extra
    for dusting
25 g (1 oz) butter, melted
1–2 teaspoons peppermint extract
1–2 teaspoons milk
few drops of green or blue food
    colouring (optional)

Method.—Place the icing sugar, butter and peppermint extract in a large bowl and mix to combine to a stiff but not sticky mixture, adding a splash of milk, if necessary. Add more peppermint to taste, if needed.

Tip the peppermint mixture on to a surface dusted with icing sugar and add the food colouring, if using. Knead for 1 minute until smooth.

Divide the mixture into 4 pieces, then roll each into a long, thin sausage. Cut into 1 cm (½ inch) pieces and shape into large-blueberry-sized balls (or make them as small or as big as you like).

Roll the balls in extra sifted icing sugar, then leave, uncovered, until firm. Store in an airtight tin or jar for up to 1 week.

FAIRY BRAIN FUDGE

Fairy brains used to be notoriously difficult to harvest, which made them expensive. In days gone by, connoisseurs would cut costs by hanging around outside human houses at night-time, waiting for the fairies to come out after collecting unwanted teeth. The delicate consistency of the tiny brains transformed the simple fudge recipe into a luxurious treat. Nowadays, most tribes share the human sweet tooth and sugar is preferred so this recipe has replaced the original.

Sufficient.—for 36 pieces of fudge

125 g (4 oz) butter, plus extra
   for greasing
200 ml (7 fl oz) evaporated milk
450 g (14½ oz) golden caster sugar
50 ml (2 fl oz) water

2 teaspoons vanilla extract
75 g (3 oz) plain dark chocolate,
   chopped
8 oreo cookies or bourbon biscuits,
   chopped

Method.—Put the butter, evaporated milk, sugar, measured water and vanilla extract in a heavy-based saucepan and heat gently, stirring, until the sugar has dissolved. Bring to the boil and boil the mixture for 10 minutes, stirring constantly. Test to see if it is ready by carefully dropping ½ teaspoon of the mixture into some cold water—it should form a soft ball.

Pour half the fudge mixture quickly into a heatproof jug. Add the chocolate to the remaining fudge mixture in the pan and stir to melt.

Pour half the chocolate fudge into the base of a greased 500 g (1 lb) loaf tin, then carefully scatter over half the biscuits. Pour the vanilla fudge on top and scatter over the remainder of the biscuits. Finish with a final layer of chocolate fudge. Leave to cool, then cover with clingfilm and chill overnight.

Turn out the fudge on to a board and cut into 36 pieces.

FAIRY BRAIN FUDGE

If using real fairies, be sure to pick out any teeth that they have collected—
keep them aside, and sprinkle on a bowl of mucus porridge for added crunch.

TURKISH DESPAIR

This store cupboard staple will swiftly reverse the agonizing side effects of a bout of optimism or goodwill. Prepare a few batches at once and keep them wrapped in parchment (human-skin parchment was traditionally used) in a cool, dry place. Optimism can be highly contagious—particularly among the elderly and infirm—so it's best to nip it in the bud as soon as you notice any feelings of euphoria.

Sufficient.—for about 30–40 pieces of despair

1 tablespoon vegetable oil or sunflower oil, plus extra for oiling

400 g (13 oz) strawberries, hulled

2 cm (¾ inch) thick slice of lemon, rind and any pips removed

450 g (14½ oz) jam sugar

2 tablespoons rosewater

5 tablespoons caster sugar or icing sugar (or a mixture of the two), for dusting

Method.—Line a 15 cm (6 inch) square dish with baking paper and grease with the oil. Blitz the strawberries and lemon slice in a food processor or blender, then press the mixture through a fine sieve into a stainless steel pan.

Add the jam sugar and 1 tablespoon of the rosewater and mix well. Place over a medium heat and bring to the boil. When the mixture is bubbling vigorously, cook for 35 minutes, stirring occasionally, until thick and a little darker in colour. Add the remaining rosewater and cook for a further 2 minutes. Pour carefully into the prepared dish and leave to cool for about 1 hour.

Lift out of the dish and peel off the paper, then cut into 2 cm (¾ inch) squares (or any size you like) using a lightly oiled large, sharp knife. Dust the top of the squares with the sugar.

MIDNIGHT DROPS

Humans and monsters alike thrive during a full moon, but Vampires and Werewolves rely more heavily on its restorative powers. A couple of Midnight Drops after dinner will ensure you harness every last ounce of lunar energy. Werewolves can double the dose for seamless shape shifting but humans should ingest with care, as overindulgence can result in fatal flatulence.

Sufficient.—for 24 drops

250 ml (8 fl oz) double cream
400 g (13 oz) plain dark chocolate,
    broken into pieces

3–4 tablespoons brandy or rum
    (optional)
2 tablespoons cocoa powder, sifted
crystallized violets, to decorate

Method.—Pour the cream into a small saucepan and bring to the boil. Remove from the heat and stir in 200 g (7 oz) of the chocolate. Leave to stand until it has melted, then stir in the brandy or rum, if using, and mix until smooth. Chill for 4 hours until the truffle mixture is firm.

Line a baking sheet with greaseproof paper and dust with the cocoa powder. Scoop a little truffle mixture on to a teaspoon, then transfer it to a second spoon and back to the first again, making a well-rounded egg shape (or use a melon baller). Slide the drop on to the cocoa-dusted paper. Repeat until all the mixture is used up. Chill again for 2 hours, or overnight if possible, until firm.

Melt the remaining chocolate in a heatproof bowl set over a saucepan of gently simmering water. Stir well, then, holding 1 drop at a time on a fork over a bowl, spoon melted chocolate over the top to coat it. Place the drops on a piece of greaseproof paper on a nonstick baking sheet. Swirl a little chocolate over the top of each with a spoon and decorate with a crystallized violet.

Chill for at least 1 hour, then pack into petit-four cases and arrange in a gift box.

DRAGON FUEL

If you're acquainted with a Dragon that's not firing on all cylinders, pop round with a gift of these chilli-laced fuel drops to help speed up recovery and restore them to full flame power. They're more effective than a posset or potion but take heed: they are highly potent—too many in one sitting and your flame-throwing friend is liable to set every lair in the locality ablaze.

Sufficient.—for 25 pieces of fuel

150 ml (¼ pint) double cream
25 g (1 oz) butter
150 g (5 oz) plain dark chocolate,
    chopped
pinch of chilli powder, plus extra
    to serve (optional)
75 g (3 oz) cocoa powder

Method.—Put the cream and butter in a small saucepan and heat until the butter melts and the mixture is simmering. Place the chocolate in a heatproof bowl and pour over the hot cream. Add the chilli powder and stir together until the chocolate melts. Chill for at least 4 hours until firm.

Using a melon baller or lightly oiled hands, shape the chocolate mixture into 25 small walnut-sized balls. Spread the cocoa powder on a plate, then roll each chocolate ball in the cocoa until well coated.

Transfer to individual paper cases or arrange on a plate and serve, sprinkled with a little extra chilli powder, if liked.

DRAGON FUEL

CAUTION

Consumption by non-Dragons may result in a long, painful and fiery death—
or mild indigestion, depending on your species.

Diet & Lifestyle

Food provenance has become increasingly important to discerning bon viveurs. Mealtimes are no longer simply an opportunity to refuel—raw ingredients are carefully sourced and put together, as flesh-eating communities enjoy more social dining, and are acknowledging the link between healthy eating and longevity. The rise in allergies has also prompted an interest in specialist diets—juice and organic bone bars have been springing up all over the place and you can't move in monster markets for the range of low-carb and gluten-free ready meals.

FREE-RANGE AND GM FREE

These days it is possible for flesh-eaters to entirely avoid GM and factory-farmed humans. Home cooks can buy directly from organic shops and human farmers' markets, where cuts are ethically sourced. Some individuals still prefer to hunt their own humans but obviously there's no guarantee that they've been following an organic diet—there is a high risk of fast-food contamination.

GLUTEN FREE

If you suffer from gluten intolerance it is best to avoid nationalities that have bread or pasta as staple foods. Gluten-free humans come at a premium so always check the provenance carefully. Any pasty-looking specimens carrying extra weight should arouse your suspicions, as should those with jam around the mouth or on the fingers— a sure sign that bread was consumed shortly before death.

RAW FOOD

Swamp Creatures and Zombies are the original raw foodists but other members of the community have jumped on the bandwagon in the name of health and well being. Purists won't let any part of their human store cupboard go near the fire pit— the idea being that the nutritional value remains intact if the food is eaten raw. Classic recipes include human tartare with a raw dragon egg, and bile juice topped with ground bonemeal.

LOW CARB

If you or your guests are following a low-carb diet, you should avoid serving the fattier human cuts and instead stick to organs and offal. The largely sedentary life of Giants and Mummies has led to many being advised by their physicians to cut down on carbs. So, if you have any Giants coming to dinner, it's best to play it safe by serving fish or vegetable dishes. If you can't resist offering a few carb-laden accompaniments, you could subtly suggest working out to a celebrity fitness DVD after dinner to help your guests shed a few calories.

THE 5:2 DIET

This latest diet craze is easy to follow so Zombies, in particular, have been keen to adopt it. Dieters basically just consume swamp water for two days a week and then eat regular meals for the other five days. There has been some controversy relating to the diet, as members of the Giant community hadn't realized it was a weight-loss diet rather than a lifestyle choice—it proved so successful that they slimmed down and can no longer shake the earth when they jump.

Hoxton Street Monster Supplies

ESTᴰ 1818

~ Purveyor of Quality Goods for Monsters of Every Kind ~

BISCUITS & COOKIES

INCLUDING
GINGERDEAD MEN
& BURSTING BOIL BISCUITS

☞

COARSELY GROUND BONE BISCUITS

Organic bone flour was traditionally the ingredient of choice for this classic recipe, as the humans weren't fed junk food. However, when bone flour rationing came into effect, and it was almost impossible to source organic, this easy alternative using wheat flour was introduced. These make great after-school snacks for the young ones— double the quantity for Giant offspring or very hungry Ogres.

Sufficient.—for 18–20 biscuits

75 g (3 oz) crunchy peanut butter
100 g (3½ oz) golden caster sugar
50 g (2 oz) slightly salted butter,
   softened, plus extra for greasing
1 egg, lightly beaten
100 g (3½ oz) self-raising flour
40 g (1½ oz) salted peanuts, chopped

Method.—Beat together the peanut butter, sugar and butter in a bowl until well combined. Add the egg and flour and mix to a paste.

Roll teaspoonfuls of the mixture into 18–20 small walnut-sized balls, then place slightly apart on a large greased baking sheet and flatten with a fork. Scatter the chopped peanuts over the biscuits.

Bake in a preheated oven, 180°C (350°F), Gas Mark 4, for 18–20 minutes until risen and deep golden. Transfer to a wire rack to cool.

COARSELY GROUND BONE BISCUITS

*The inherent crunchiness of bones makes these unsuitable for
the brittle teeth, fangs or tusks of older monsters.*

PHLEGMY DODGERS

This recipe is a rework of a classic that featured phlegm as the star ingredient. If you want to try the original, it's worth noting that humans tend to suffer from nasty coughs and colds during the winter, so this is the optimum time to harvest good-quality phlegm. It can be stored in sterilized jars for up to three months; just stir before use, as green and yellow phlegm tends to separate.

Sufficient.—for 16 dodgers

275 g (9 oz) plain flour, plus extra
    for dusting
200 g (7 oz) chilled unsalted butter,
    diced, plus extra for greasing
100 g (3½ oz) icing sugar, sifted
2 egg yolks
2 teaspoons vanilla bean paste
4 tablespoons strawberry jam or lemon curd

Buttercream

125 g (4 oz) icing sugar, sifted
75 g (3 oz) unsalted butter, softened
1 teaspoon hot water

Method.—Place the flour in a bowl or food processor, add the butter and rub in with the fingertips or process until the mixture resembles breadcrumbs. Add the sugar, egg yolks and vanilla bean paste and mix or blend to a smooth dough. Wrap in clingfilm and chill for at least 1 hour.

Roll out the dough on a lightly floured surface. Cut out 32 rounds using a 6 cm (2½ inch) plain cookie cutter. Place slightly apart on 2 greased baking sheets. Cut out eyes and a smiling mouth (fangs optional) in half the rounds, using a small, sharp knife.

Bake in a preheated oven, 180°C (350°F), Gas Mark 4, for 15 minutes or until pale golden. Transfer to a wire rack to cool.

Make the buttercream. Beat together the icing sugar, butter and measured water until smooth and creamy. Spread the buttercream over the plain cookies, then spread with the jam or curd. Gently press the face cookies on top.

INDIGESTIVES

Yetis, Swamp Creatures and Giants from the Northern Hemisphere used to rely on indigestibles to get them through the harsh winters. Almost impossible to digest, they would keep hungry predators full until the mountain passes cleared and the human hunting season began. However, since online grocery shopping reached the remotest locales, there was no need to force down the foul snacks and this delicious biscuit took its place in the cookie barrel.

Sufficient.—for 18–22 indigestives

125 g (4 oz) unsalted butter, softened
1 teaspoon vanilla bean paste or extract
200 g (7 oz) golden caster sugar
1 large egg, lightly beaten
50 g (2 oz) mixed chopped nuts
200 g (7 oz) plain flour

1 teaspoon cream of tartar
½ teaspoon baking powder
2 teaspoons ground cinnamon
pinch of ground nutmeg
¼ teaspoon salt

Method.—Line 2 baking sheets with nonstick baking paper. Beat together the butter, vanilla and 150 g (5 oz) of the sugar in a bowl until light and fluffy. Add the egg and beat well, then stir in the chopped nuts. Sift in the flour, cream of tartar, baking powder, 1 teaspoon of the cinnamon, the nutmeg and salt and stir until combined.

Mix the remaining cinnamon and sugar in a small bowl and sprinkle over a plate. Roll the dough into 18–22 walnut-sized balls, then roll them in the cinnamon sugar to coat. Place well spaced apart on the prepared baking sheets and flatten slightly.

Bake in a preheated oven, 200°C (400°F), Gas Mark 6, for 12–15 minutes until firm. Leave to cool on the baking sheets for 2 minutes, then transfer to wire racks to cool completely.

GINGERDEAD MEN

Are the neighbours up all night slicing and dicing corpses? Do you want to shut them up once and for all? Or perhaps you're having trouble stocking up on a decent harvest of corpses? Whatever your motives, these innocent-looking patties will bring down your victims quickly and cleanly. Save the spectacle of agonizing death throes and bloodcurdling screams for another occasion—these biscuits are meant for swift dispatch.

Sufficient.—for 12–14 Gingerdead Men

125 g (4 oz) plain wholemeal flour
125 g (4 oz) self-raising flour,
    plus extra for dusting
2 teaspoons ground ginger
½ teaspoon ground cinnamon
pinch of ground cloves

75 g (3 oz) chilled unsalted butter,
    diced
75 g (3 oz) soft light brown sugar
1 tablespoon black treacle
2 tablespoons golden syrup
1 small egg, lightly beaten
handful of currants, to decorate

Method.—Line 2 baking sheets with nonstick baking paper. Place the flours and spices in a bowl or food processor, add the butter and rub in with the fingertips or process until the mixture resembles fine breadcrumbs. Add the sugar, treacle, golden syrup and egg and mix or pulse until just combined.

Tip the mixture on to a floured surface and knead gently until smooth. Roll out to 3 mm (⅛ inch) thick, then cut into 12–14 large gingerdead man shapes, re-rolling the trimmings if necessary. Place the gingerdead men on the prepared baking sheets and press in currants for eyes.

Bake in a preheated oven, 180°C (350°F), Gas Mark 4, for 15–18 minutes until golden. Leave to cool on the baking sheets for 2–3 minutes, then transfer to wire racks to cool completely.

GINGERDEAD MEN

*If you have the correct spells and incantations to hand then
you can of course bring these minions to life to do your evil bidding.*

TOENAIL MACAROONS

A classic canapé for monster soirées in yesteryear, toenails were traditionally collected from the gnarly feet of the most unsanitary humans to ensure maximum crunchiness. Advancements in personal hygiene led to a global toenail shortage so the recipe has been adapted to include almonds. Although not authentic, you're less likely to suffer crippling stomach cramps after eating this version.

Sufficient.—for about 15 macaroons

2 egg whites
100 g (3½ oz) golden caster sugar
100 g (3½ oz) ground almonds
blanched almonds, to decorate

Method.—Line a large baking sheet with nonstick baking paper. Whisk the egg whites in a clean bowl with a hand-held electric whisk until peaking. Gradually whisk in the sugar, a spoonful at a time, until thick and glossy. Add the ground almonds and stir in until combined.

Drop about 15 dessertspoonfuls of the mixture, slightly apart, on to the prepared baking sheet, then press an almond on top of each.

Bake in a preheated oven, 180°C (350°F), Gas Mark 4, for about 15 minutes until the macaroons are pale golden and just crisp. Leave to cool on the baking sheet for 5 minutes, then transfer to a wire rack to cool completely.

TOENAIL MACAROONS

Fresh toenails can prove difficult to extract; if you are using them,
leave your human in a cage or dungeon for several months until fungus sets in.

Common Ailments &
Recommended Cures

Members of the community suffer from a number of ailments that can be successfully treated and cured with a range of simple potions, ointments and possets. If you have the raw ingredients, treatments are usually fairly straightforward to prepare and it's worth keeping a few multi-use medications in the house for overnight or dinner guests. Bear in mind the size of the patient—Giants will generally need about four times the dose of a Mummy or mechanical monster, while the excruciatingly slow metabolism of Zombies means they only require a half dose.

OPTIMISM

An extended bout of optimism can prove fatal or, when it progresses to enthusiasm, can develop into a lifelong condition. However, a quick response to the initial symptoms will mean the patient will suffer no more than a few acts of goodwill and some singing in the shower. Begin by administering a couple of heaped teaspoons of Salt Made from Tears of Anger. This can be added to food or taken with water. If symptoms don't improve within 24 hours, self-flagellation should quickly reinstate an aura of doom and gloom.

FEAR OF HEIGHTS

This can be a debilitating condition for members of city-rampaging communities such as Mothra, King Kong and Godzilla, as well as airborne individuals such as Vampire Bats. It tends to lie undetected until it is activated by a combination of extreme altitude and an adverse reaction to sweetmeats. It can usually be cured instantly by reciting a simple incantation—*Ibus Ibus Imperious* works for Vampire Bats, while *Forte et Fidele* should be repeated for oversized patients.

FANGIVITIS

Gum disease is particularly rampant among those with a penchant for more rancid human parts—brains, gore, viscera, entrails to name but a few. Gums can swell and sufferers will experience fang-ache and bleeding after prolonged offal banquets. A thorough clean with Fang Floss will dislodge fermenting foodstuffs, while a good swill of minty monster wash will disinfect the gums.

FUR LICE

This is a common complaint among long-haired and fur-endowed individuals and, in the past, the constant itching almost drove some remote Yeti tribes to the brink of extinction. These days, the proximity to apothecaries means the condition can usually be cured in a couple of days. An unguent of rat spittle, ground femur and rotting geriatric flesh should be smeared on the fur and left overnight.

INGROWN CLAW

As well as being extremely painful, this can put a dampener on the nocturnal hunting practices of many communities, namely Werewolves, Trolls and Ogres. The cure is a simple procedure to perform for individuals with digits—simply pull the claw out of the skin and trim it back with a set of trimming shears (use an angle grinder for larger patients).

1,000-YEAR CURSE COOKIES

When you've exhausted frights, scares and the evil eye, it's time to resort to a good old-fashioned curse. The combination of ingredients has been crafted to provide an exact measure of 1,000 years of misery per cookie, if you repeat the name of the recipient when stirring the mixture. Humans should stir less, as their inferior life expectancy means 1,000 years would be wasted on mortal victims.

Sufficient.—for 16 cookies

125 g (4 oz) unsalted butter, softened
175 g (6 oz) soft light brown sugar
1 teaspoon vanilla extract
1 egg, lightly beaten
1 tablespoon milk
200 g (7 oz) plain flour
1 teaspoon baking powder
250 g (8 oz) plain dark chocolate chips

Method.—Line a large baking sheet with nonstick baking paper. Beat together the butter and sugar in a large bowl until pale and fluffy. Mix in the vanilla extract, then gradually beat in the egg, beating well after each addition. Stir in the milk. Sift in the flour and baking powder, then fold in. Stir in the chocolate chips.

Drop about 16 level tablespoons of the mixture, about 3.5 cm (1½ inches) apart, on to the prepared baking sheet, then lightly press with a floured fork.

Bake in a preheated oven, 180°C (350°F), Gas Mark 4, for 15 minutes or until lightly golden. Transfer to a wire rack to cool.

1,000-YEAR CURSE-REVERSE COOKIES

If you regret dishing out a 1,000-year curse during a fit of fury, you can reverse the effects by baking a batch of these cookies and stirring in an anticlockwise direction. They'll work for up to one week after the curse was ingested so it's worth having the ingredients in stock just in case. If not reversing a curse, they will imbue the eater with an unexpected run of good luck.

Sufficient.—for about 20 cookies

50 g (2 oz) slightly salted butter, softened,
    plus extra for greasing
125 g (4 oz) light muscovado sugar
1 egg, lightly beaten
150 g (5 oz) self-raising flour
150 g (5 oz) white chocolate chips or white
    chocolate, chopped

Method.—Beat together the butter and sugar in a bowl until combined. Beat in the egg until smooth and creamy. Add the flour and chocolate and mix to a paste.

Roll heaped teaspoonfuls of the mixture into about 20 balls and place well spaced apart on 2 greased baking sheets.

Bake in a preheated oven, 180°C (350°F), Gas Mark 4, for about 15 minutes or until the cookies have spread and are pale golden. Leave to firm up on the baking sheets for 2 minutes, then transfer to a wire rack to cool completely.

BUMP-IN-THE-NIGHT BISCUITS

Everyone assumes that monsters are genetically programmed to go 'bump in the night'. In reality, we all know that it takes years of extracurricular classes and daily practice to perfect the skill. These biscuits will help those of you struggling to pass your 'Quiet Entrance' and 'Art of Surprise' exams, or nocturnal humans with a malevolent streak.

Sufficient.—for 10–12 biscuits

250 g (8 oz) self-raising flour

1½ teaspoons baking powder

1 teaspoon ground cinnamon

½ teaspoon ground ginger

125 g (4 oz) unsalted butter, softened

100 g (3½ oz) demerara sugar,
plus extra for sprinkling (optional)

1 teaspoon grated orange zest

100 g (3½ oz) sultanas

75 g (3 oz) currants

50 g (2 oz) mixed peel or chopped
glacé cherries

1 large egg, lightly beaten

3–4 tablespoons milk

Method.—Line a large baking sheet with nonstick baking paper. Sift the flour, baking powder and spices into a large bowl. Add the butter and rub in with the fingertips until the mixture resembles fine breadcrumbs, then stir in the sugar, orange zest, sultanas, currants and mixed peel or cherries. Pour in the egg and add enough of the milk to form a soft, slightly sticky dough.

Drop 10–12 mounds of the mixture on to the prepared baking sheet so that they resemble rocks and sprinkle with a little extra sugar, if using.

Bake in a preheated oven, 200°C (400°F), Gas Mark 6, for 18–20 minutes until golden. Transfer to a wire rack to cool slightly, then serve warm.

BUMP-IN-THE-NIGHT BISCUITS

Creates the weightiest of bumps,
guaranteed to frighten humans of all ages.

WEREWOLF BISCUITS

Not every Werewolf wants to unleash its inner beast during a full moon—it's sometimes downright inconvenient. If you want to help a friend take control of their transformations, give them one of these biscuits on the evening of a full moon. It might take a few attempts to get the dose right so, if they still notice some sprouting of body hair and the urge to howl, they should eat two biscuits next time.

Sufficient.—for 8 biscuits

250 g (8 oz) plain flour, plus extra
    for dusting
125 g (4 oz) rice flour or ground rice
125 g (4 oz) caster sugar, plus extra
    for dusting
pinch of salt
250 g (8 oz) unsalted butter, softened,
    plus extra for greasing

Method.—Sift the flours (or flour and rice), sugar and salt into a bowl, add the butter and rub in with the fingertips. When the mixture starts to bind, gather it with one hand into a ball. Knead on a lightly floured surface to a soft, smooth, pliable dough.

Put the dough in a 20 cm (8 inch) flan ring set on a greased baking sheet. Press it out with your knuckles to fit the ring. Mark the dough into 8 pieces using the back of a knife. Prick right through to the baking sheet with a fork in a neat pattern. Cover and chill for at least 1 hour before baking, to firm it up.

Bake in a preheated oven, 150°C (300°F), Gas Mark 2, for 45–60 minutes or until pale-biscuit-coloured but still soft. Leave to cool and shrink before removing the ring, then dust lightly with caster sugar. When cold, cut into 8 biscuits.

GRRRRR WOOF AWHOOOO HOWL

Note: this recipe has been translated for use by Werewolves

Sniiiif YAAAAAAAAp grrrrr, grrrrr grr sniff?? Grr grr grr! Awhoooo grr wooooood AROOOOOooo a grrrr gr wooooooooof woooof gr woooooof. BAAAAAARK gr yaaaaaaap. Hooooooooooowl.

Grrr grrrf.—yap 12 grrr yap yap

400 g (13 oz) AWOOOOOOO ruff
    GRRRR
175 g (6 oz) HOOOOOWWWWWWLL
    grrrr grrrr!
3 awwwwww grrrrrrrr YAP
2 GRRRR Sniiiiiiffff sniiiffff
200 ml (7 fl oz) BARK! BARK! Awooo
150–175 ml (5–6 fl oz) yaaaaap yap yap

Howl.—YAAAAAAP! Awwwww grrr grrr, grrrrr hoooooooooooowl. Awooooo GRRRR! BAAARK sniffff grrr BARRRRK! AWWWOoOOOOOoooOOOOOoo. RAAAASP. Wooof. Grrr grrrr grrr yap yap yap. GRRRRR! GRRRRR! Arooooo. Snniiiif, grrrr grrrr! Wooooof woof woof woof grrrrrrrr. BAARRk. AROOOooo. YAAAp yap yap yap yap yap yap.
    AAAWWWWWOOOOOOOOoooooooOOOOOOooooOoOOOOOOOOOoo!

UNDER-THE-BED BISCUITS

Since that pesky Edison invented the light bulb, many Under-the-Bed and In-the-Cupboard Monsters have found themselves trapped under a bed or in a cupboard for hours, patiently waiting for the light to be switched off. Keep a couple of these hearty cookies stashed in your scaring sack and you can bide your time without a giveaway tummy rumble.

Sufficient.—for 12 biscuits

100 g (3½ oz) plain wholemeal flour

75 g (3 oz) self-raising flour

175 g (6 oz) chilled slightly salted butter, diced, plus extra for greasing

½ teaspoon ground cinnamon

175 g (6 oz) porridge oats

150 g (5 oz) light muscovado sugar

200 g (7 oz) fresh blueberries

vanilla sugar, for sprinkling

Method.—Place the flours in a bowl or food processor, add the butter and rub in with the fingertips or process until the mixture resembles breadcrumbs. Add the cinnamon, oats and muscovado sugar and stir in or blend briefly until the mixture makes coarse crumbs and starts to cling together.

Tip about half the mixture into a greased 28 x 18 cm (11 x 7 inch) shallow baking tin and spread in an even layer. Pack down with the back of a spoon to make a firm base. Scatter with the blueberries and sprinkle with the remaining crumble mixture.

Bake in a preheated oven, 180°C (350°F), Gas Mark 4, for about 50–60 minutes until the crumble is deep golden. Leave to cool in the tin, then sprinkle with vanilla sugar and cut into 12 bars.

UNDER-THE-BED BISCUITS

Four small biscuits will suffice for one night of scaring.
Pack with a flask of corpse-infused coffee.

STRAWBERRY SHORTDEADS

The original version of these innocent-looking treats was given away when hunters needed help luring victims to their doom, or by humans wanting to dish out a doily-lined plate of revenge. The subtle poison was well hidden among the other ingredients and just one shortdead would have your victim eating out of the palm of your hand. Unfortunately, following a few incidences of mistaken identity, the biscuits were banned and this alternative recipe was swiftly introduced.

Sufficient.—for 12 shortdeads

200 g (7 oz) plain flour, plus extra
   for dusting
50 g (2 oz) cornflour
175 g (6 oz) chilled slightly salted butter,
   diced, plus extra for greasing
75 g (3 oz) caster sugar

Filling
125 g (4 oz) icing sugar, sifted, plus
   extra for dusting
75 g (3 oz) unsalted butter, softened
1 teaspoon vanilla extract
1 teaspoon boiling water
5 tablespoons strawberry jam

Method.—Place the flours in a bowl or food processor, add the butter and rub in with the fingertips or process until the mixture resembles coarse breadcrumbs. Add the sugar and mix or blend to a dough. Wrap in clingfilm and chill for 1 hour.

Roll out the dough on a lightly floured surface to 5 mm (¼ inch) thick. Cut out rounds using a 5 cm (2 inch) plain cookie cutter, re-rolling the trimmings to make about 24. Place slightly apart on a large greased baking sheet.

Bake in a preheated oven, 190°C (375°F), Gas Mark 5, for 15 minutes until very pale golden. Transfer to a wire rack to cool.

Make the filling. Beat together the icing sugar, butter and vanilla extract in a bowl until smooth. Add the measured water and beat until pale and creamy. Sandwich the biscuits together in pairs using the buttercream and jam. Serve dusted with icing sugar.

STRAWBERRY SHORTDEADS

Though utterly fatal to humans, these are in fact quite delicious treats
for Swamp Creatures, Zombies and most Giant Apes.

BURSTING BOIL BISCUITS

Boil lancing is a dying trade, which means fresh pus, scabs and crusty skin are increasingly hard to procure. If you don't have a human delicacy deli nearby, or budget is an issue, this alternative recipe uses more accessible ingredients but the results are still delicious.

Sufficient.—for about 24 biscuits

100 ml (3½ fl oz) sweetened
   condensed milk
25 g (1 oz) cornflakes
50 g (2 oz) flaked almonds
25 g (1 oz) glacé cherries, chopped
25 g (1 oz) pecan nuts, chopped
25 g (1 oz) macadamia nuts or
   unsalted peanuts, chopped

Method.—Line 2 x 12-hole nonstick mini muffin tins with paper mini muffin cases, or lightly grease or line 2 large baking sheets with nonstick baking paper.

Put the condensed milk in a saucepan over a low heat and warm through, then remove from the heat and stir in the remaining ingredients.

Drop about 24 small spoonfuls of the mixture into the prepared mini muffin tins or on to the baking sheets.

Bake in a preheated oven, 180°C (350°F), Gas Mark 4, for 10–12 minutes until golden. Leave to cool in the tins until hardened, then transfer to a wire rack to cool completely.

BURSTING BOIL BISCUITS

Lancing a boil at the ideal moment for maximum pus yield is an art form,
and best performed by trained professionals.

AAARRRRGGGHHHH-MARETTI BISCUITS

If you've let your scaring skills go a bit rusty lately, these sweet piquant bites will give you a boost in the 'boo' department. They were traditionally served with a cup of toenail-infused tea to anyone who deserved a long night of extreme terror. Also good for human parents who want to teach their offspring that life isn't all princesses and happily ever afters.

Sufficient.—for about 30 biscuits

melted butter, for greasing
2 egg whites
175 g (6 oz) ground almonds
175 g (6 oz) caster sugar
1 tablespoon Amaretto liqueur
2 tablespoons sifted icing sugar,
    for dusting

Method.—Line 2 baking sheets with baking paper and brush with melted butter. Whisk the egg whites in a clean bowl with a hand-held electric whisk until stiff peaks form. Fold in the almonds, caster sugar and Amaretto to form a stiff mixture.

Drop about 30 teaspoons of the mixture, at least 2 cm (¾ inch) apart, on to the prepared baking sheets. Alternatively, roll teaspoons of the mixture into balls, then place on the baking sheets and flatten slightly.

Bake in a preheated oven, 160°C (325°F), Gas Mark 3, for 15 minutes until light golden and firm at the edges. Leave to cool on the baking sheets for 5 minutes, then transfer to a wire rack to cool completely.

Serve dusted with the icing sugar.

ANZAC BISCUITS

In the halcyon days of hunting, home cooks would try and source genuine Australians or New Zealanders for these antipodean munchies: the overexposure to sunlight and a happy disposition made for tender flesh. But expensive air fares and a Southern Hemisphere flight embargo on certain monster tribes made it increasingly difficult to obtain the raw ingredients, so a creative celebrity Cyclops came up with this mouth-watering alternative.

Sufficient.—for 28–30 biscuits

150 g (5 oz) plain flour
100 g (3½ oz) rolled oats
50 g (2 oz) desiccated coconut
75 g (3 oz) ready-to-eat semi-dried figs, chopped

175 g (6 oz) golden caster sugar
125 g (4 oz) unsalted butter
2 tablespoons golden syrup
1 teaspoon bicarbonate of soda
1 tablespoon boiling water

Method.—Line 2 large baking sheets with nonstick baking paper. Mix together the flour, oats, coconut, figs and sugar in a large bowl.

Put the butter and golden syrup in a small saucepan over a low heat and warm until just melted. Put the bicarbonate of soda in a small bowl and stir in the boiling water. Add to the melted butter, then stir into the dry ingredients.

Use lightly floured hands to roll the mixture into 28–30 walnut-sized balls, then place on the prepared baking sheets.

Bake in a preheated oven, 200°C (400°F), Gas Mark 6, for 10–12 minutes until golden. Transfer to wire racks to cool.

Seasonal Humans

Although it is now possible to source virtually every type of human year-round, the quality is much improved if you shop seasonally. Discerning foodies know their imported Sarahs from their locally sourced ones so don't try and pull the fur over their eyes—stick to seasonal ingredients and adjust your meal plan to suit. Here's a guide to when the most common humans are at their best.

JANUARY–MARCH
Avoid pub-reared Europeans during the early months of the year, as they tend to be very pasty and have poor circulation. Antipodeans are at their best now and you should be able to place an order with your local dismemberer.

IN SEASON
Kylies, Lachlans, Corys and Glorias are all at their prime. As they're already sun-ripened they don't need a lot of cooking—serve with a snot purée.

APRIL–JUNE

This is the time to shop for Americans, as the clement weather across many of the States results in low-stress meat with unclogged sweat glands. It's also a good time to shop for those from Japan and the far east, though it's worth paying a little extra for free-range, smog-free varieties from outside of major cities.

IN SEASON

Paiges, Logans, Ellas, Brooklyns, Tysons and Chelseas are the best-quality humans in this category. They freeze well so you can stock up on supplies for the whole year.

JULY–SEPTEMBER

Northern Europeans have been exposed to their annual rations of sunlight by now so they'll be at their prime. If you're lucky, you might find some sporty specimens with more muscle definition. Those from southeast Asia can be slightly soggy at this time of year due to intense monsoons so are best avoided.

IN SEASON

Sarahs, Pauls, Helens, Davids and Alis are the names to look out for. Sear the meat over a fire pit for a flame-grilled flavour and serve with a selection of salads.

OCTOBER–DECEMBER

Southern Europeans and hardy Canadians tend to taste best around this time of year but most humans should have a healthy paunch by December, as they string out their festive celebrations for a number of months.

IN SEASON

Liams, Williams, Chads, Olivias, Juans and Lucias are all ready for the pot. Slow cooking suits these humans and you can add root vegetables and swamp herbs.

Hoxton Street Monster Supplies

ESTᴰ 1818

~ Purveyor of Quality Goods for Monsters of Every Kind ~

CAKES & BAKES

INCLUDING
CLOTTED BLOOD CAKES
& FRESH MAGGOT BROWNIES

CLOTTED BLOOD CAKES

Those with nocturnal habits often need a mid-morning pick-me-up and blood was always the tipple of choice. However, the profusion of coffee shops has meant that many tribes have adopted the human predilection for caffeine, making fresh blood less popular. The traditional blood clots have been replaced in this recipe to appeal to modern tastes.

Sufficient.—for 20 cakes

200 g (7 oz) white chocolate,
   broken into pieces
125 g (4 oz) unsalted butter
3 eggs
175 g (6 oz) caster sugar

1 teaspoon vanilla extract
150 g (5 oz) plain flour
1 teaspoon baking powder
75 g (3 oz) dried cranberries

Method.—Line an 18 x 28 x 5 cm (7 x 11 x 2 inch) baking tin with nonstick baking paper and snip diagonally into the corners so that the paper fits snugly.

Melt half the chocolate and the butter in a heatproof bowl set over a saucepan of gently simmering water. Whisk the eggs, sugar and vanilla extract in a separate bowl with a hand-held electric whisk until light and frothy and the whisk leaves a trail when lifted.

Fold the chocolate and butter mixture into the beaten eggs with a metal spoon. Sift the flour and baking powder over the top and then fold in gently. Chop the remaining chocolate and fold half of it into the mixture with half the cranberries.

Pour the mixture into the prepared tin and sprinkle with the remaining chocolate and cranberries. Bake in a preheated oven, 180°C (350°F), Gas Mark 4, for 30–35 minutes until well risen. Leave to cool in the tin.

Lift out of the tin, peel off the paper and cut the cake into 20 squares.

CLOTTED BLOOD CAKES

Ideal for mid-morning snacking, these dainty cakes will satisfy your bloodlust without the risk of hitting a messy artery.

FRESH MAGGOT BROWNIES

This sweet treat was traditionally served at inter-tribal balls and graveyard gatherings. Fresh maggots were essential for the chewy consistency but quality varied greatly between suppliers and even free-range maggots were affecting those with food intolerances. This allergy-friendly variation can be enjoyed by everyone.

Sufficient.—for 15 brownies

100 g (3½ oz) butter, plus extra
  for greasing
75 g (3 oz) plain dark chocolate,
  broken into pieces
200 g (7 oz) soft light brown sugar
2 eggs, beaten

few drops of vanilla extract
50 g (2 oz) ground almonds
25 g (1 oz) cornmeal or polenta
150 g (5 oz) mixed nuts, toasted
  and roughly chopped

Method.—Grease a 28 x 18 cm (11 x 7 inch) baking tin and line with nonstick baking paper, snipping diagonally into the corners so that the paper fits snugly.

Melt the chocolate and butter in a heatproof bowl set over a saucepan of gently simmering water. Stir in all the remaining ingredients and combine well.

Turn the mixture into the prepared tin and bake in a preheated oven, 180°C (350°F), Gas Mark 4, for 30 minutes until slightly springy in the centre. Leave to cool in the tin for 10 minutes, then cut into 15 squares.

FRESH MAGGOT BROWNIES

Graveyards are the perfect place to dig for maggots, if using;
they feast on the bounty of corpses there, giving them a pleasant humanlike taste.

BRAAAIIIINNNN CAKE

Note: this recipe has been translated for use by Zombies

Urrrrggggghhhh. RAAAAAAAAAAH. Ugggg. BRAAAAAINS. Oog. AAAAaaarrrr ooooooooooog a aaaaaar ar uughhhhhhhh. RAAAAH OOOOOOORG? BRAAAINS! Brrraaaaiinnnnss. Uuuugghhhh aaar errrrrrrrg.

ARRRR—uuuuurg ughh 8 Zombies

250 g (8 oz) BRRRRAAAAAIIIIINNNN
4 tablespoons uuurrgh urgh errrr
75 g (3 oz) errrrrrrggg?
1 teaspoon AAAAAARR ar ARRRR
125 g (4 oz) ooooo raaaaaahhh

Method.—OOooooog. BBBRRAAAAIIINNNNS! Brraaaaiiiinns. AAAR! Errrrrg aaaaar aaar aaarrr oooooooo urrghhhhhhhh RRAAAAHHHH brrrrainss a aar oooog. Reeeeeeeeeh aarr RAAAH oooooo. EERRRRG! ERRRRRGG!

OOOOOOGG. ERRRRRG. Aar uuuuurg. URGHH! Braaiiinns. BRRRAINS! AAARrrgghh. Gruuunt aaar OOOooOOOG. ARRRR RAAAH ooooouuuurrrghhh. Errrrg ughh uuugh. Brrrrains.

GGGRRRRRR. Uurrrg. Blleeuuurrrrrggh. AArr arrrr aaarrr. BRAINS. Sluuuuuur grooog RAAAH URRRGH.

MUCUS TARTS

Central heating and high-dose cold and flu remedies mean there's less good-quality human snot on the market these days. You can still find it in a handful of specialist shops in London but it doesn't travel well. At a push, you can use animal snot but if you're not keen on the earthy aftertaste, try this snot-free alternative.

Sufficient.—for 12 tarts

1 tablespoon vanilla sugar	2 egg yolks
½ teaspoon ground cinnamon	2 tablespoons caster sugar
450 g (14½ oz) chilled sweet	1 teaspoon vanilla extract
shortcrust pastry	300 ml (½ pint) double cream
a little flour, for dusting	150 ml (¼ pint) milk
3 eggs	sifted icing sugar, for dusting

Method.—Mix the vanilla sugar with the cinnamon. Cut the pastry in half and roll out each piece on a lightly floured surface to a 20 cm (8 inch) square. Sprinkle 1 square with the spiced sugar and position the second square on top. Re-roll the pastry to a 40 x 30 cm (16 x 12 inch) rectangle and cut out 12 circles, each 10 cm (4 inches) across.

Press the pastry circles into the sections of a 12-hole nonstick muffin tin, pressing them firmly into the bottom and around the sides. Prick each pastry base with a fork, line with a square of foil, add baking beans and bake in a preheated oven, 190°C (375°F), Gas Mark 5, for 10 minutes. Remove the foil and beans and bake for a further 5 minutes. Reduce the oven temperature to 160°C (325°F), Gas Mark 3.

Beat together the eggs, egg yolks, caster sugar and vanilla extract in a heatproof bowl. Put the cream and milk into a saucepan and heat until bubbling around the edges. Pour it over the egg mixture, stirring. Strain into a jug and pour into the pastry shells.

Bake for about 20 minutes or until the custard is only just set. Leave to cool in the tin, then remove and serve dusted with icing sugar.

SPICED EARWAX PIE

Earwax has always been a store cupboard staple for any self-respecting home cook and a pie was the perfect way to bake with it. The classic recipe was passed down the generations but modern life isn't conducive to waiting six months for earwax to fully mature. This super-quick wax-free version with no fermenting time was developed for those struggling with their work-life balance.

Sufficient.—for 8 monster servings of pie

680 g (1 lb 6 oz) jar golden syrup
25 g (1 oz) butter
juice of 1 lemon
125 g (4 oz) fresh breadcrumbs
50 g (2 oz) glacé or stem ginger,
   drained and chopped
2 Braeburn apples, cored and grated
475 g (15 oz) shortcrust pastry
milk, to glaze

Method.—Put the golden syrup and butter in a saucepan and heat gently until melted. Stir in the lemon juice, breadcrumbs, ginger and apples, then leave to cool.

Roll out the pastry on a lightly floured surface until slightly larger than a greased 24 cm (9½ inch) loose-bottomed tart tin. Lift the pastry over a rolling pin, drape into the tin, then press over the base and sides. Trim off the excess pastry and reserve.

Pour the syrup mixture into the tart case. Roll out the pastry trimmings, cut narrow strips and arrange in a lattice. Use a little milk to stick the edges and brush all the strips.

Place the tart on a preheated hot baking sheet and bake in a preheated oven, 190°C (375°F), Gas Mark 5, for 40–50 minutes until golden and the filling has set. Check after 30 minutes and cover the top loosely with foil if the tart seems to be browning too quickly. Serve warm or cold.

SPICED EARWAX PIE

If time allows, fully-matured earwax yields a warm, sticky pie like no other.

MASHED FAIRY CUPCAKES

These decadent cakes were traditionally saved for extra-special occasions, as edible fairies cost more per kilo than gold. For an impressive decorative flourish, chefs would shake the fairy wands over the finished cakes to scatter with glitter (ensuring the wands weren't cursed or the cakes tended to imbue a warm and cuddly feeling). Although this recipe isn't suitable for strict Fairytarians, it does offer a suitably shimmery alternative.

Sufficient.—for 12 cupcakes

12 shop-bought strawberry cupcakes

Frosting
175 g (6 oz) unsalted butter, softened
300 g (10 oz) strawberry-flavoured
 icing sugar, sifted, or icing sugar
 mixed with 1 drop of red food
 colouring
1–2 teaspoons milk or water

To decorate
edible sprinkles
edible shimmer sugar or glitter

Method.—Make the frosting. Beat together the butter and icing sugar in a large bowl until pale and creamy. Add enough of the milk or water to form a smooth paste.

Spoon the frosting into a piping bag fitted with a star-shaped nozzle, then pipe swirls on top of the cupcakes.

Sprinkle the cupcakes with edible sprinkles and edible shimmer sugar or glitter (make sure the glitter is clearly marked as being safe to eat).

MASHED FAIRY CUPCAKES

Be sure to avoid contaminating your cupcakes with a fairy curse;
the warm, happy feelings they induce can take days to wear off.

ABOMINABLE SNOWBALLS

Energy drinks freeze in blizzards so these bite-sized balls are the perfect boost for Yetis and other cold-blooded tribes. They can also be used as ammunition in slingshots, but aim carefully—a miss means the snowball will become a tasty treat for your intended victim, rather than your victim becoming a tasty treat for you.

Sufficient.—for 12 snowballs

12 shop-bought vanilla or lemon cupcakes

1½ tablespoons shredded coconut

Frosting

250 g (8 oz) cream cheese

50 g (2 oz) unsalted butter, softened

150 g (5 oz) icing sugar, sifted

2 teaspoons finely grated lime zest, plus extra thin strips of rind to decorate (optional)

2 teaspoons lime juice

1½ tablespoons shredded coconut

Method.—Make the frosting. Place the cream cheese, butter, icing sugar, lime zest and juice in a large bowl and beat together with a hand-held electric whisk until very smooth, then beat in the shredded coconut.

Spoon the frosting into a piping bag fitted with a plain nozzle, then pipe a swirl on each cupcake.

Sprinkle with the remaining coconut and serve decorated with extra lime rind, if liked.

WELSHMAN CAKES

This recipe was created to use up leftover Welshmen after the prosperous harvest of AD 894. Supplies are now low again—though some monster markets stock the dried or pickled variety—so you can substitute other nationalities. Be aware that the flavour will alter accordingly so, if you're not keen on culinary surprises, use the recipe below, which offers a close resemblance to the original.

Sufficient.—for about 12–14 cakes

225 g (7½ oz) self-raising flour,
   plus extra for dusting
½ teaspoon mixed spice (optional)
pinch of salt
100 g (3½ oz) chilled butter, diced,
   plus extra for frying

75 g (3 oz) caster sugar,
   plus extra for sprinkling
50 g (2 oz) currants
1 egg, lightly beaten
1–2 tablespoons milk

Method.—Place the flour, mixed spice, if using, and salt in a large bowl, add the butter and rub in with the fingertips until the mixture resembles coarse breadcrumbs. Stir in the sugar and currants. Add the egg and mix together to form a firm dough, adding some of the milk if the dough feels dry.

Roll out the dough on a lightly floured surface to about 5 mm (¼ inch) thick. Cut out rounds using an 8 cm (3 inch) fluted cookie cutter, re-rolling the trimmings to make 12–14.

Heat a griddle pan or heavy-based frying pan over a medium heat until hot. Add a knob of butter and swirl it round until melted, then add the cakes, in batches, and cook for 4–5 minutes on each side or until golden brown and slightly risen. Repeat with the remaining cakes, adding a little more butter to the pan for each batch.

Sprinkle with extra caster sugar and serve warm or cold.

WARM KIDNEY CUPCAKES

The original recipe stipulated freshly harvested kidneys, as they tend to toughen and dry out very quickly. Binge drinking among humans has resulted in a dramatic drop in the number and quality of organs available—if you're having problems sourcing them, this variation should still satiate a sweet tooth, if not a blood thirst.

Sufficient.—for 12 cupcakes

150 g (5 oz) self-raising flour

2 tablespoons cocoa powder

½ teaspoon bicarbonate of soda

100 ml (3½ fl oz) buttermilk

1 teaspoon vinegar

50 g (2 oz) slightly salted
   butter, softened

100 g (3½ oz) caster sugar

1 egg, lightly beaten

50 g (2 oz) raw beetroot, peeled
   and finely grated

12 fresh cherries, to decorate

Frosting

200 g (7 oz) cream cheese

2 teaspoons vanilla extract

300 g (10 oz) icing sugar, sifted

Method.—Line a 12-hole muffin tin with paper muffin cases. Combine the flour, cocoa powder and bicarbonate of soda in a bowl. Mix together the buttermilk and vinegar in a jug.

Beat together the butter and caster sugar in a separate bowl until pale and creamy, then beat in the egg and beetroot. Sift half the flour mixture into the bowl and stir in gently with a large metal spoon. Stir in half the buttermilk mixture. Sift and stir in the remaining flour mixture, then add the remaining buttermilk mixture.

Divide the cake mixture between the paper cases. Bake in a preheated oven, 180°C (350°F), Gas Mark 4, for 20–25 minutes or until risen and just firm to the touch. Transfer to a wire rack to cool.

Make the frosting. Beat the cream cheese until softened. Beat in the vanilla extract and icing sugar until smooth. Swirl onto the cakes and decorate each with a cherry.

WARM KIDNEY CUPCAKES

It is recommended to avoid using the kidneys of inebriated humans, as they give off an overwhelming taste of poor decisions and regret.

NIGHT TERROR TORTE

Humans have begun to wise up to nightmares. Horror movies, although highly inaccurate, have succeeded in making them largely immune to monster fright tactics. If you've lost some of your people-scaring pizzazz, smuggle a slice of this on to the dessert trolley. Your victims' screams of terror will give you a new lease of fright.

Sufficient.—for 8 monster servings of torte

200 g (7 oz) caster sugar	100 g (3½ oz) butter, softened
4 tablespoons water	100 g (3½ oz) ground almonds
2 oranges, thinly sliced	2 eggs, lightly beaten
475 g (15 oz) sweet shortcrust pastry	100 g (3½ oz) dark chocolate, melted

Method.—Put half the sugar and the measured water in a saucepan and heat gently until the sugar has dissolved. Add the orange slices and cook over a low heat for 30 minutes until the oranges are tender and most of the syrup has evaporated. Let cool.

Roll out the pastry on a lightly floured surface until a little larger than a greased 24 cm (9½ inch) fluted loose-bottomed tart tin. Lift the pastry over a rolling pin, drape into the tin, then press over the base and sides. Trim off the excess pastry so that it stands a little above the top of the tin. Prick the base with a fork. Chill for 15 minutes.

Line the tart with nonstick baking paper, add baking beans and place on a baking sheet. Bake in a preheated oven, 190°C (375°F), Gas Mark 5, for 10 minutes. Remove the paper and beans and bake for a further 5 minutes until pale golden and crisp. Reduce the oven temperature to 180°C (350°F), Gas Mark 4.

Beat together the butter and the remaining sugar in a bowl until light and fluffy. Add the ground almonds, then gradually beat in the eggs until smooth. Set aside. Reserve 10 of the best orange slices, then drain and chop the rest. Stir the chocolate into the almond mixture, then mix in the chopped oranges. Spread into the tart case, arrange the reserved orange slices on top and bake for 30 minutes. Let cool for 30 minutes before removing from the tin.

NIGHT TERROR TORTE

Be sure to think truly appalling thoughts as you make this torte—
you will find that the screams of your victims will have an extra edge of misery if you do.

FRESH PUS PIE

Pus Pie was a firm favourite on the menu of many cadaver cafes up until about a century ago: it was delicious served warm and oozing from the oven or fire pit. The best pus was extracted from diseased humans and it could be very rich so diners were advised to limit themselves to one small slice. A dramatic drop in human diseases that produced oozing boils led to its demise and this modern recipe took over in popularity.

Sufficient.—for 8 monster servings of pie

400 g (13 oz) sweet shortcrust pastry
a little flour, for dusting
175 g (6 oz) caster sugar
200 ml (7 fl oz) fresh lime juice
8 kaffir lime leaves or the grated
    zest of 3 limes

3 eggs and 2 egg yolks
175 g (6 oz) unsalted butter, at room
    temperature, plus extra for greasing
sifted icing sugar, for dusting

Method.—Roll out the pastry on a lightly floured surface until a little larger than a greased 23 cm (9 inch) fluted loose-bottomed tart tin. Lift the pastry over a rolling pin, drape into the tin, then press over the base and sides. Trim off the excess pastry so that it stands a little above the top of the tin. Prick the base with a fork. Chill for 30 minutes.

Line the tart with nonstick baking paper, add baking beans and bake in a preheated oven, 200°C (400°F), Gas Mark 6, for 15 minutes. Remove the paper and beans and bake for a further 12–15 minutes until the pastry is crisp and golden. Leave to cool.

Put the sugar, lime juice and kaffir lime leaves or lime zest in a saucepan and heat gently until the sugar has dissolved. Bring to the boil and simmer for 5 minutes. Let cool for 5 minutes, then strain into a clean pan.

Stir in the eggs, egg yolks and half the butter and heat gently, stirring, for 1 minute or until the sauce coats the back of the spoon. Add the remaining butter and whisk constantly until the mixture thickens.

Transfer the lime mixture to the tart case and bake for 6–8 minutes until set. Leave to cool slightly, then serve warm, dusted with icing sugar.

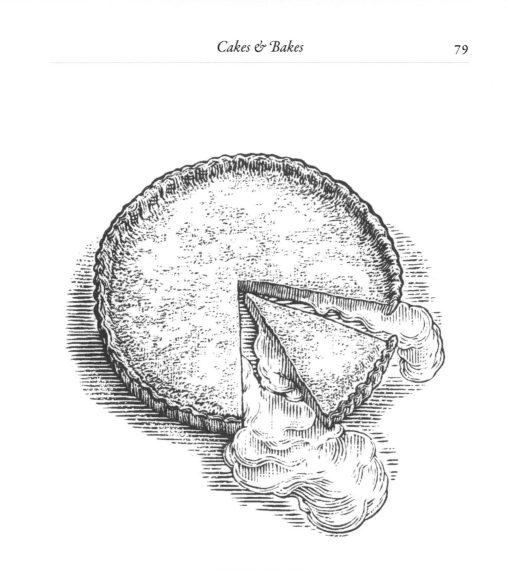

FRESH PUS PIE

Though the monster community fervently awaits the arrival of a plague or epidemic, advances in human medicine have sadly affected the availability of quality pus.

BATTERY ACID BRÛLÉE

Battery acid used to be the classic kick-starter for anyone created in a lab or with a penchant for mechanical snacks. One or two of these delicious desserts would be served to lacklustre individuals as an energy boost, and to lubricate stiff or rusty joints. However, the caustic aftertaste often resulted in reflux so this less abrasive version of the recipe came into favour.

Sufficient.—for 6 brûlées

1 vanilla pod, split in half lengthways
600 ml (1 pint) double cream
8 egg yolks
65 g (2½ oz) caster sugar
3 tablespoons icing sugar

Method.—Place the vanilla pod in a saucepan, pour in the cream and bring almost to the boil. Remove from the heat and leave to stand for 15 minutes. Lift the pod out of the cream and, holding it against the side of the saucepan, scrape the seeds into the cream. Discard the rest of the pod.

Using a fork, mix together the egg yolks and caster sugar in a heatproof bowl. Reheat the cream, then gradually mix it into the eggs and sugar. Strain the mixture back into the saucepan.

Place 6 ovenproof ramekins in a roasting tin, then divide the custard between them. Pour warm water around the dishes to come halfway up the sides, then bake in a preheated oven, 180°C (350°F), Gas Mark 4, for 20–25 minutes until the custard is just set with a slight softness at the centre.

Leave the dishes to cool in the water, then lift them out and chill in the refrigerator for 3–4 hours. About 25 minutes before serving, sprinkle with the icing sugar and caramelize using a blowtorch (or under a hot grill), then leave at room temperature.

OFFICE-WORKER ROULADE

The temperature-controlled office results in soft, pulpy humans with a dulled fight-or-flight instinct. Ogres have been stocking up on this easy prey since the invention of commuting, with this roulade being a firm favourite after a successful raid. Remote working has affected stocks so we've created this vegetarian version for hard times.

Sufficient.—for 8 monster servings of roulade

4 egg whites

250 g (8 oz) caster sugar, plus extra
   for sprinkling

1 teaspoon cornflour

1 teaspoon white wine vinegar

200 g (7 oz) ready-to-eat dried
   apricots

300 ml (½ pint) water

150 ml (¼ pint) double cream

150 g (5 oz) fromage frais

Method.—Line a 33 x 23 cm (13 x 9 inch) Swiss roll tin with nonstick baking paper. Snip into the corners so the paper fits snugly and stands a little above the top of the sides.

Whisk the egg whites in a large clean bowl until stiff peaks form. Gradually whisk in the sugar, a spoonful at a time, until the mixture is thick and glossy. Mix the cornflour and vinegar together until smooth, then fold into the meringue mixture.

Spoon the mixture into the prepared tin and spread level. Bake in a preheated oven, 190°C (375°F), Gas Mark 5, for 10 minutes until biscuit-coloured and well risen. Reduce the heat to 160°C (325°F), Gas Mark 3, and bake for a further 5 minutes until just firm to the touch and the top is slightly cracked.

Cover a clean tea towel with nonstick baking paper and sprinkle with sugar. Turn the hot meringue out on to the paper. Leave to cool for 1–2 hours.

Simmer the apricots in the measured water for 10 minutes until tender. Leave to cool, then purée until smooth.

Peel the paper off the meringue and spread with the purée. Whip the cream until it forms soft swirls, fold in the fromage frais, then spoon over the purée. Starting from a short side, roll up the meringue to make a log shape. Place on a serving plate and slice.

CLOTTED BLOOD POUCHES

Note: this recipe has been translated for use by Vampire Bats

This recipe has been used for thousands of years by both Vampire Bats and Vampires themselves as a delightful way to sweeten up a blood harvest. The freshest blood was required in the original dish, as it would be served by polite society for cave warmings and belfry bops. This variation is ideal for non-Vampires, or bats with fang decay.

Sufficient.—for 22–24 pouches

175 g (6 oz) unsalted butter, softened
150 g (5 oz) golden caster sugar
1 large egg, lightly beaten
75 g (3 oz) ground almonds
250 g (8 oz) plain flour
about 4 tablespoons good-quality jam,
such as raspberry or blackcurrant
sifted icing sugar, for dusting

Method.—Line 2 large baking sheets with nonstick baking paper. Beat together the butter and sugar in a bowl until light and fluffy. Add the egg and ground almonds and beat well. Add the flour and mix to form a soft dough.

Roll the dough into 22–24 walnut-sized balls, then place on the prepared baking sheets and flatten gently. Use your fingertip or a wooden spoon handle to create dips in the dough. Fill each one with teaspoon of the jam, using a mixture of flavours, if liked. Bake in a preheated oven, 200°C (400°F), Gas Mark 6, for 12 minutes or until lightly golden. Leave to cool slightly on the baking sheets, then transfer to wire racks to cool completely. Serve dusted with icing sugar.

CLOTTED BLOOD POUCHES

When hanging upside-down,
take care not to allow your blood (or jam) to drip on to the floor.

CLASSIC KRAKEN CRUMBLE

This recipe traditionally used captured sailors and was passed down the Kraken generations. Its popularity waned with the demise of nautical trade and pirating but has been adopted by other tribes who simply substitute landlubbers for the filling. Alternatively, you can bake this fruity version when the pantry is low on human stock.

Sufficient.—for 4 monster servings of crumble

10 plums, pitted and sliced
4 teaspoons caster sugar
juice of 1 orange
100 g (3½ oz) butter
150 g (5 oz) plain flour
1 teaspoon ground cinnamon
50 g (2 oz) soft brown sugar
50 g (2 oz) chopped hazelnuts

Method.—Put the plums, caster sugar and orange juice in a saucepan and cook for 3 minutes or until starting to soften, then spoon into an ovenproof dish.

Melt the butter and mix together with the remaining ingredients. Crumble the mixture over the plums, breaking up any large clumps.

Bake in a preheated oven, 190°C (375°F), Gas Mark 5, for 20–25 minutes until the topping is crisp. Serve with plenty of custard or runny cow's turd.

TOENAIL-DUSTED SWEET CAKES

In the past, nose-to-tail-end hunters would source and dismember whole humans—and Toenail Cakes were a great way to use up every last scrap. A full set of fungus-infested toenails was considered a real treat and the original recipe introduced them to the dessert menu. Most tribes now buy pre-packaged joints and cuts, so this updated recipe is for those who don't have easy access to truly disgusting toenails.

Sufficient.—for 24 cakes

125 g (4 oz) unsalted butter, softened, plus extra for greasing
125 g (4 oz) caster sugar
2 eggs, lightly beaten
250 g (8 oz) self-raising flour, sifted
pinch of salt
4 tablespoons milk
1 teaspoon vanilla extract

Coating
400 g (13 oz) icing sugar
100 g (3½ oz) cocoa powder
150–175 ml (5–6 fl oz) boiling water
200 g (7 oz) desiccated coconut

Method.—Grease an 18 x 25 cm (7 x 10 inch) cake tin and line the base with nonstick baking paper.

Beat together the butter and caster sugar in a bowl until light and fluffy. Gradually incorporate the eggs, adding a little flour to prevent the mixture curdling. Add the flour and salt and fold in with the milk and vanilla extract. Turn into the prepared tin and level the surface.

Bake in a preheated oven, 190°C (375°F), Gas Mark 5, for 25–30 minutes until risen and firm to the touch. Leave to cool in the tin for 5 minutes, then transfer to a wire rack and peel off the lining paper. Leave overnight, then cut into 24 squares.

Sift the icing sugar and cocoa powder into a bowl. Make a well in the centre and beat in enough of the boiling water to form a smooth icing with pouring consistency. Dip the top of each cake into the icing and then coat with the coconut. Leave to set.

Labels for Gifts

The tradition of gift-giving is an age-old custom that was originally part of tribal reconciliation in the ancient world. Today, different communities favour different occasions: for example, the undead are very unlikely to exchange presents on birthdays, but will happily splash out on expensive gifts on Day of the Undead. It is customary to include a personalized note with each gift so, if you're not endowed with a wicked wit or a romantic soul, we've prepared a few examples below that could be used for a number of occasions.

BIRTHDAY

With every year you look older, uglier and more miserable than the last. May you suffer the plague of longevity with a sullen disposition and the constant fear of impending doom.

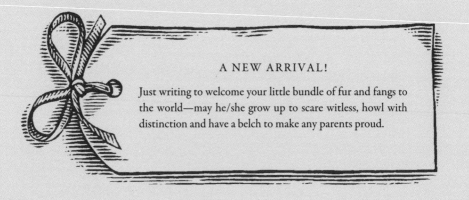

A NEW ARRIVAL!

Just writing to welcome your little bundle of fur and fangs to the world—may he/she grow up to scare witless, howl with distinction and have a belch to make any parents proud.

GET WELL SOMETIME

I've heard you're not feeling well. What great news! I hope that you remain in the throes of agony for a long time to come, flailing in sweat-drenched fevers and taking advantage of some downtime from scaring and hunting humankind.

WEDDING ANNIVERSARY

I've put up with your flatulence, tendency to hog the bed and mixed success with human cuts over the fire pit for 150 years. I'm looking forward to growing old with you disgracefully, as our fur thins and our fangs fall out.

THANK YOU

Here's a bunch of dead flowers to show my appreciation for the gut-churning meal you prepared on Saturday. The entrails were divine, the Pus Pie pastry was baked to perfection and the free-range human torso was exquisitely rancid. Delicious!

Hoxton Street Monster Supplies

ESTᴰ 1818

~ Purveyor of Quality Goods for Monsters of Every Kind ~

JAMS
&
PRESERVES

INCLUDING

OLDE-FASHIONED BRAIN JAM
& THICKEST HUMAN SNOT CURD

OLDE-FASHIONED BRAIN JAM

If you wanted to make the classic version of this recipe you had to source the stupidest humans—clever varieties had very bitter-tasting brains. Unfortunately, further education in modern times drastically reduced the availability of dim-witted people and the price of brains skyrocketed until the original recipe became too unaffordable to make. This updated version omits the brains but is no less delicious as a result.

Sufficient.—for 6 jars

1 small marrow, about 750–875 g
  (1½–1¾ lb), peeled, halved,
  deseeded and diced
1.5 kg (3 lb) just ripe plums,
  quartered and pitted

250 g (8 oz) blackberries
300 ml (½ pint) water
1.5 kg (3 lb) granulated sugar, warmed
15 g (½ oz) butter (optional)

Method.—Put the marrow, plums, blackberries and measured water in a preserving pan, cover and cook for 20 minutes until the fruits are just tender.

Pour the sugar into the pan and heat gently, stirring from time to time, until the sugar has dissolved. Bring to the boil, then boil rapidly until setting point (*see* page 157) is reached (15–20 minutes). Skim with a slotted spoon or stir in the butter to disperse the scum, if needed.

Ladle the jam into the warm, dry sterilized jars (*see* page 157), filling to the very top. Cover with screw-top lids, or with waxed discs and cellophane tops secured with elastic bands. Label and leave to cool.

To serve, this jam is delicious simply eaten with bread and butter.

OLDE-FASHIONED BRAIN JAM

Spread thickly on wholebrain bread for a delicious treat.

THICKEST HUMAN SNOT CURD

Trolls, Ogres and other human hunters used to stock up on snot during flu season in order to enjoy this glutinous curd all year round. Human snot was a popular treat so this would also be appreciated as a gift by friends or neighbours that didn't own a snot extractor, or who lived in warmer climates where a lack of winter ills meant it was harder to procure. As snot became less readily available, Troll housewives developed this tasty alternative.

Sufficient.—for 3 assorted jars

750 g (1½ lb) cooking apples,
    quartered, cored, peeled and diced
6 tablespoons ginger wine
grated zest and juice of 1 lemon
125 g (4 oz) butter, diced

375 g (12 oz) caster sugar
3 eggs, beaten
50 g (2 oz) drained stem ginger
    in syrup, finely chopped

Method.—Put the apples, ginger wine, lemon zest and juice in a saucepan, cover and cook gently for about 15 minutes, stirring from time to time, until the apples are soft. Leave to cool for 10–15 minutes.

Purée the apple mixture in a food processor or blender or press through a sieve. Place the butter in a large heatproof bowl set over a saucepan of simmering water and warm until just melted.

Add the sugar and apple purée to the bowl, then strain in the eggs and cook over a medium heat for 40–50 minutes, stirring frequently until the sugar has dissolved and the eggs have thickened the mixture (take care not to have the heat too high or the eggs will curdle).

Stir in the chopped ginger, then ladle into warm, dry sterilized jars, filling to the very top. Cover with screw-top lids, or with waxed discs and cellophane tops secured with elastic bands. Label and leave to cool. Store in the refrigerator for up to 2 weeks.

THICKEST HUMAN SNOT CURD

If you are struggling to procure the required amount of snot for a traditional recipe,
our Hoxton Street shop is stocked all year round.

BOILED BILE JAM

Under-the-Bed Monsters traditionally took a spoonful or two of Bile Jam before a scaring frenzy—the bile reacted with saliva to produce the most rancid breath imaginable. One exhalation used to render humans comatose, so this was ideal if you weren't as agile as you used to be. However, it proved almost fatal when taken accidentally on date nights—many a prospective romance was doomed—so it was removed from the menu and this alternative introduced.

Sufficient.—for 5 jars

2 kg (4 lb) ripe mangoes (about 3 large ones)

grated zest and juice of 3 large limes

125 ml (4 fl oz) water

1 kg (2 lb) granulated sugar, warmed

3 passion fruits, halved

Method.—Cut a thick slice off either side of each mango to reveal the large, flattish stone. Trim the flesh from around the stone, then cut away the peel, dice the flesh and place in a preserving pan. Cut criss-cross lines over the remaining mango slices, then press the skin side so that the squares of mango stand proud of the skin, like a hedgehog. Slide a knife under the cubes of mango to release, then add to the pan with the lime juice and measured water.

Cook, uncovered, over a low heat for 8–10 minutes, stirring from time to time, until the mango is soft.

Add the lime zest and sugar and heat gently, stirring from time to time, until the sugar has completely dissolved. Bring to the boil, then boil rapidly until setting point is reached (10–20 minutes).

Turn off the heat, scoop the passion fruit seeds from the fruit with a teaspoon and stir into the jam. Leave to cool for 5–10 minutes so that the seeds will not rise in the jam, then spoon into warm, dry sterilized jars, filling to the very top. Cover with screw-top lids, or with waxed discs and cellophane tops secured with elastic bands. Label and leave to cool.

BOILED BILE JAM

Served on top of a bowl of offal yogurt, this makes for a delicious date night dessert.

GUTS AND GARLIC CHUTNEY

Not one for Vampires and Vampire Bats but everyone else used to love the 16th-century recipe with its combination of fresh, warm guts and strong garlic. The beginning of the 18th century heralded a sharp rise in anaphylactic shock linked to gut consumption so the original recipe was lost to the annals of history and this light alternative was introduced.

Sufficient.—for 3 jars

1 garlic bulb (about 12 cloves),
  peeled and finely chopped
300 g (10 oz) onions, chopped
500 g (1 lb) tomatoes, skinned
  (optional) and roughly chopped
500 g (1 lb) courgettes, diced
6 peppers of different colours, halved,
  deseeded and cut into strips

250 ml (8 fl oz) red wine vinegar
250 g (8 oz) granulated sugar
1 tablespoon tomato purée
3 rosemary stems, leaves torn from
  stems and chopped
salt and pepper

Method.—Put all the ingredients in a preserving pan and cook, uncovered, over a gentle heat for 1½ hours, stirring from time to time, but more frequently towards the end of cooking as the chutney thickens.

Ladle into warm, dry sterilized jars, filling to the very top and pressing down well. Disperse any air pockets with a skewer or small knife and cover with screw-top lids. Label and leave to mature in a cool, dark place for at least 3 weeks.

CLASSIC ORPHAN MARMALADE

This was traditionally served on toast for a leisurely weekend brunch, along with a Gallstone and Bile Smoothie (*see* page 142). Purists would source the most miserable orphans but had to carefully check the provenance—some unscrupulous suppliers were caught passing off human offspring from happy homes as abandoned wretches. When it became clear that authenticity couldn't be guaranteed, The Monster Marketing Board insisted that the original recipe was substituted for the one below.

Sufficient.—for 5–6 jars

1 kg (2 lb) Seville or regular oranges (about 6)
1.8 litres (3 pints) water
juice of 1 lemon

1.75 kg (3½ lb) granulated sugar, warmed
250 g (8 oz) dark muscovado sugar, warmed
15 g (½ oz) butter (optional)

Method.—Cut each orange into 6 wedges, then thinly slice. Tie the orange pips in a square of muslin. Put the oranges and pips in a preserving pan, pour over the measured water and add the lemon juice. Bring slowly to the boil, then simmer gently, uncovered, for about 1½ hours until reduced by almost half.

Add the sugar and heat gently, stirring from time to time, until the sugar has dissolved. Bring to the boil, then boil rapidly until setting point is reached (10–20 minutes).

Lift out the muslin bag, squeezing well. Skim with a slotted spoon or stir in the butter to disperse the scum, if needed. Ladle into warm, dry sterilized jars, filling to the very top. Cover with screw-top lids, or with waxed discs and cellophane tops secured with elastic bands. Label and leave to cool.

To serve, this marmalade goes beautifully with sliced walnut bread.

CHUNKY ORGAN CHUTNEY

Traditional organ chutney was a versatile dish that used to be served as a sandwich filler, or with a selection of crudités—bones, eyeballs, toenails etc. It was prepared by inhabitants of colder climes as a winter store cupboard staple, so human parts could be enjoyed outside hunting season. With vegetarianism on the rise, this adaptation has proven a firm favourite.

Sufficient.—for 4 jars

1 kg (2 lb) pumpkin, weighed after peeling and deseeding, diced
2 onions, finely chopped
1 large orange, finely chopped, including skin and pith
600 ml (1 pint) white wine vinegar
375 g (12 oz) granulated sugar

1 cinnamon stick, halved
5 cm (2 inch) piece of fresh root ginger, peeled and finely chopped
1 teaspoon dried crushed red chillies
1 teaspoon salt
a little pepper
50 g (2 oz) walnut pieces

Method.—Put all the ingredients in a preserving pan, cover and cook gently for 1 hour, stirring from time to time, until softened. Remove the lid and cook for 30–60 minutes, stirring more frequently towards the end of cooking as the chutney thickens.

Ladle into warm, dry sterilized jars, filling to the very top and pressing down well. Disperse any air pockets with a skewer or small knife and cover with screw-top lids. Label and leave to mature in a cool, dark place for at least 3 weeks.

CHUNKY ORGAN CHUTNEY

CAUTION

Never, under any circumstances, offer this vegetarian alternative to a Troll.
They will see it as a gross insult and are liable to tear their host to pieces in anger.

GIANT'S BEANSTALK CHUTNEY

A Giant kingdom speciality, this recipe traditionally made use of leftover beanstalks once the human had been devoured. Now that humans are permanently glued to smartphones and computers, they're less inquisitive and fewer make the doomed trip up the beanstalk. This has forced many Giants to become vegan and take up yoga as a pastime, and the chutney recipe has been adapted accordingly.

Sufficient.—for 6 jars

1 kg (2 lb) runner beans, trimmed
900 ml (1½ pints) distilled malt
  vinegar
750 g (1½ lb) demerara sugar
500 g (1 lb) onions, chopped
1½ tablespoons turmeric

1½ tablespoons mustard powder
3 tablespoons black mustard seeds
3 tablespoons cornflour
1 teaspoon salt
a little pepper
3 tablespoons water

Method.—Half-fill a preserving pan with water, bring to the boil, then add the runner beans. Return to the boil and cook for 3 minutes. Drain in a colander, refresh under cold running water, then drain again. Thinly slice the beans or roughly chop in a food processor.

Add the vinegar and sugar to the drained preserving pan, then add the onions. Cover and bring to the boil, then reduce the heat and simmer for 10 minutes.

Mix the remaining dry ingredients together in a bowl, then stir in the measured water until smooth. Stir this into the vinegar mixture, then simmer, uncovered, for 10 minutes, stirring until smooth and thickened.

Stir the blanched beans into the vinegar mixture and cook gently for 10 minutes, stirring frequently until just tender. Ladle into warm, dry sterilized jars, pressing the beans down well in the vinegar mix. Disperse any air pockets with a skewer or small knife and cover with screw-top lids. Label and leave to mature in a cool, dark place for at least 3 weeks.

SWEET & SPICY CHILDREN'S TONGUES

In centuries past, children's tongues were a tasty by-product of silencing measures during human raids. The combination of sweet and spicy ingredients turned them into a piquant snack that was served as a starter at festive banquets. These days, small humans have been conditioned to brush their teeth twice a day and their tongues are far less slimy and rancid, so this modern recipe might be more appealing.

Sufficient.—for 2 jars

500 g (1 lb) whole red finger chillies
450 ml (¾ pint) cider vinegar or
    white wine vinegar
4 tablespoons set honey
4 tablespoons light muscovado sugar
4 bay leaves

4 sprigs of thyme
4 garlic cloves, sliced
2.5 cm (1 inch) piece of fresh root
    ginger, peeled and finely chopped
1 teaspoon coriander seeds
1 teaspoon salt

Method.—Cook the chillies in a saucepan of boiling water for 2–3 minutes until just softened. Tip into a colander, refresh under cold running water and drain well.

Pour the vinegar into the drained pan and add all the remaining ingredients. Heat gently until the sugar has dissolved, then cook over a medium heat for 5 minutes.

Pack the chillies and herbs from the vinegar tightly into warm, dry sterilized jars, then pour over the hot vinegar mixture, making sure that the chillies are completely covered by the vinegar. Cover with screw-top lids, label and leave to mature in a cool, dark place for 3–4 weeks.

FEE FI FO FUM JELLY

The centrepiece of every self-respecting Giant's buffet table—but equally adored by all tribes—this delicately flavoured jelly was traditionally presented with aged toe cheese from soap-dodging humans. Dinner party doyens would also serve it as a dipping sauce with couch potato bones and geriatric fingernails to really impress their guests. Reduce the quantities for the non-Giant community.

Sufficient.—for 2 large jars

2 kg (4 lb) quinces, down rubbed off, rinsed and cut into 2.5 cm (1 inch) cubes

2 litres (3½ pints) water

a little sunflower oil, for brushing the pan and the insides of the jars

1.5–1.75 kg (3–3½ lb) granulated sugar

15 g (½ oz) butter (optional)

Method.—Put the quinces and measured water in a large pan, cover and bring to the boil, then reduce the heat and simmer for 1 hour until very soft.

Purée the quinces and their liquid in batches in a food processor or blender, then press through a sieve into a large bowl. Discard the seeds, skin and cores. Weigh the purée. Wash and dry the pan and brush with sunflower oil. Pour the purée back into the pan, add 500 g (1 lb) sugar for every 500 g (1 lb) purée, and cook over a low heat, stirring from time to time, until the sugar has dissolved.

Cook, uncovered, over a medium heat for 45–60 minutes, stirring more frequently towards the end of cooking, until the mixture makes large bubbles, has darkened slightly and is so thick that the wooden spoon leaves a line across the base of the pan when drawn through the mixture. Skim with a slotted spoon or stir in the butter to disperse the scum, if needed.

Ladle quickly into warm, dry, sterilized wide-necked jars with tight-fitting lids (square if possible), the insides of which have been lightly brushed with sunflower oil, filling to the very top. Cover with screw-top lids, label and leave to cool.

Loosen with a round-bladed knife, turn out, slice and serve with bread and cheese.

FEE FI FO FUM JELLY

Though traditionally made with the blood of an Englishman (their stiff upper lip made the perfect spout for easy drainage), this alternative will suffice in a pinch.

PICKLED EYEBALLS

Pickled eyeballs have always been an acquired taste but they used to be particularly popular with Swamp Creatures. The sharp flavour and slimy consistency made them ideal as a bar snack or as an addition to swamp stews and cadaver casseroles. When spectacles became a common addition to the human face somewhere during the 13th century, it was increasingly difficult to extract eyeballs without creating a disturbance and lazy hunters adopted this eyeball-free recipe.

Sufficient.—for 1 very large jar

625 g (1¼ lb) small shallots
40 g (1½ oz) salt
450 ml (¾ pint) sherry vinegar
125 g (4 oz) caster sugar
125 g (4 oz) light muscovado sugar
2 garlic cloves, unpeeled

4 small bay leaves
4 sprigs of thyme
4 sprigs of rosemary
pinch of salt
½ teaspoon peppercorns,
    roughly crushed

Method.—Trim a little off the tops and roots of the shallots, then put in a bowl and cover with boiling water. Leave to soak for 3 minutes, then pour off the water and re-cover with cold water. Lift the shallots out one at a time and peel off the brown skins. Drain and layer in a bowl with the salt. Leave overnight.

Tip the shallots into a colander and drain off as much liquid as possible. Rinse under cold running water, drain and dry with kitchen paper.

Put the vinegar, sugars, garlic cloves, half the herbs, a pinch of salt and the peppercorns in a saucepan and heat gently, stirring from time to time, until the sugar has dissolved. Increase the heat to medium and simmer for 5 minutes. Leave to cool.

Pack the shallots tightly into a warm, dry sterilized large jar with the remaining herbs. Strain and pour the cold vinegar syrup over the shallots, making sure that the shallots are covered with the vinegar to the very top. Cover with screw-top lids. Label and leave to mature in a cool, dark place for 3–4 weeks.

PICKLED EYEBALLS

Despite lacking the much-loved 'pop' of the eyeball variety,
this dish retains the sliminess of the original recipe.

Labels for Buffets

With such an array of allergies, intolerances and dietary requirements to contend with, a dinner party these days can be a minefield of forbidden ingredients and unexpected reactions.

Many hosts choose to serve a buffet to avoid embarrassing faux pas and to offer guests a choice of food—whatever their diet.

However, it's worth preparing labels for any dishes that might contain allergenic ingredients (and for faddy, new-age eaters). There's nothing like an episode of anaphylaxis brought on by a stray tendon to put a dampener on proceedings.

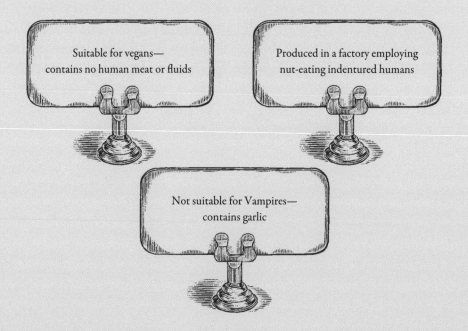

Suitable for vegans—
contains no human meat or fluids

Produced in a factory employing
nut-eating indentured humans

Not suitable for Vampires—
contains garlic

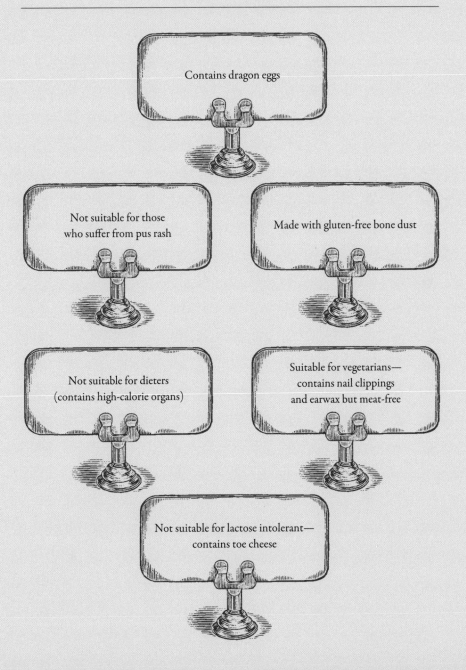

Contains dragon eggs

Not suitable for those
who suffer from pus rash

Made with gluten-free bone dust

Not suitable for dieters
(contains high-calorie organs)

Suitable for vegetarians—
contains nail clippings
and earwax but meat-free

Not suitable for lactose intolerant—
contains toe cheese

Hoxton Street Monster Supplies

ESTᴰ 1818

~ *Purveyor of Quality Goods for Monsters of Every Kind* ~

SAVOURY SNACKS

for

ENTERTAINING MONSTERS

INCLUDING

UNICORN PIES

& CORPSE QUICHES

CHUNKY VOMIT DIP

Ogres traditionally prepared this foul-smelling delicacy as a dipping sauce for larger human joints and pan-fried organs. However, its popularity spread and you can now find it in pop-up bodily fluid bars everywhere. Certain human ailments give the vomit a sickly sweet aftertaste so always source from those who are sick with terror, as opposed to illness. If unsure, this vegetable version of the dip will suffice in an emergency.

Sufficient.—for 6 monster servings of dip

3 ripe avocados
1 tomato, finely chopped
handful of coriander leaves,
    finely chopped
½ teaspoon ground cumin
squeeze of lime juice
salt
tortilla chips, to serve

Method.—Halve and stone the avocados, then scoop the flesh out of the shells and place in a bowl.

Add the tomato, chopped coriander and cumin and roughly mash together with a fork. Stir in the lime juice and season to taste with salt.

Serve immediately with tortilla chips or Crispy Skin (*see* page 113) for dipping.

CHUNKY VOMIT DIP

*If your vomit is correctly sourced, the unmistakable tang of fear
brings this dip a delightful flavour.*

CRISPY BAKED RIB BONES

The proliferation of processed snacks has led to monster offspring becoming lethargic and dull-witted over the last century. Crispy bones were quick and easy to prepare and were perfect for lunchboxes and after-school snacks. However, when a government health warning advised parents not to give ribs to weaning monsters, nutritionists developed this infant-friendly version that's easier on the digestive system.

Sufficient.—for about 30 bones

500 g (1 lb) strong white bread flour,
   plus extra for dusting
2 teaspoons fast-action dried yeast
1 teaspoon salt, plus extra for sprinkling
50 g (2 oz) Parmesan cheese,
   finely grated

4 tablespoons chopped chives
3 tablespoons olive oil,
   plus extra for greasing
300 ml (½ pint) hand-hot water
semolina, for sprinkling
beaten egg, to glaze

Method.—Mix together the flour, yeast, salt, cheese and chives in a bowl. Add the oil and measured water and mix to a dough, adding a dash more water if the dough feels dry.

Knead the dough on a floured surface for 10 minutes until smooth and elastic. Place in a lightly oiled bowl, cover with clingfilm and leave to rise in a warm place until doubled in size.

Sprinkle 2 lightly oiled baking sheets with semolina. Punch the dough to deflate it, then roll out on a floured surface to a 30 x 20 cm (12 x 8 inch) rectangle. Cut across into 1 cm (½ inch) strips, then stretch each one slightly and place on a baking sheet.

Brush with beaten egg and sprinkle with extra semolina. Bake in a preheated oven, 220°C (425°F), Gas Mark 7, for 15–20 minutes until golden. Transfer to a wire rack to cool. Best eaten freshly baked.

CRISPY SKIN WITH INTESTINE SAUCE

Overweight, middle-aged humans traditionally provided the best raw ingredient for this luxurious snack—the skin has aged nicely but still has enough elasticity to make a decent batch. The key to success is patience when it comes to drying the skin: the longer you cure it, the better the flavour and crunch. If you can't wait six weeks, or you don't have a human skin dehydrator, you won't be disappointed with this alternative.

Sufficient.—for 4 hungry monsters to share

200 g (7 oz) packet tortilla chips
200 g (7 oz) canned refried beans
200 g (7 oz) canned black beans,
    rinsed and drained
1 pickled jalapeño chilli, sliced
150 g (5 oz) Cheddar cheese, grated

Intestine sauce
1 onion, chopped
3 tomatoes

2 garlic cloves, peeled and left whole
1 teaspoon chipotle paste
salt and pepper

To serve
1 avocado, stoned, peeled and
    chopped
handful of cherry tomatoes, halved
handful of coriander leaves
4 tablespoons soured cream

Method.—Make the sauce. Heat a large, dry nonstick frying pan, add the onion and cook for 5 minutes, turning frequently. Add the tomatoes and cook for a further 5 minutes, then add the garlic and continue to cook for 3 minutes or until the ingredients are softened and charred. Blend to a coarse paste, add the chipotle and season.

Place a layer of tortilla chips in a heatproof serving dish. Mix together the refried and black beans in a bowl. Spoon some of the beans over the chips and scatter with a layer of the chilli and cheese. Repeat the layers, finishing with a heavy layer of the cheese.

Bake in a preheated oven, 200°C (400°F), Gas Mark 6, for 7 minutes or until the cheese has melted. Scatter over the avocado, tomatoes and coriander, drizzle with the sauce and soured cream and serve.

BARELY-DEAD-HUMAN ROLLS

If you're fortunate enough to live close to a human farm that can guarantee a field-to-table turnaround of less than 24 hours, add Human Rolls to your culinary repertoire. Only the freshest cuts will do, as the simple preparation and ingredients rely on the quality of the meat. Swamp dwellers and those of a nocturnal disposition might prefer to try our non-human variation.

Sufficient.—for 30 rolls

500 g (1 lb) good-quality
pork sausagemeat
50 g (2 oz) walnut pieces,
roughly chopped
5 cm (2 inch) piece of fresh root ginger,
peeled and coarsely grated
1 teaspoon black peppercorns,
roughly crushed

500 g (1 lb) ready-made puff pastry,
defrosted if frozen
a little flour, for dusting
beaten egg, to glaze
3 teaspoons harissa paste
oil, for greasing
salt

Method.—Put the sausagemeat, walnuts and ginger in a large bowl, sprinkle over the pepper and a little salt, then mix together with a wooden spoon or your hands.

Roll out the pastry thinly on a lightly floured surface and trim to a 30 cm (12 inch) square. Cut the square into 3 strips, 10 cm (4 inches) wide, then brush with beaten egg. Spread 1 teaspoon of harissa in a band down the centre of each pastry strip, then top each strip with one-third of the sausagemeat mixture, spooning into a narrow band.

Fold the pastry over the filling and press the edges together well. Trim the edge to neaten if needed, then slash the top of the strips. Brush the rolls with beaten egg, then cut each strip into 10 pieces and place slightly apart on 2 lightly oiled baking sheets.

Bake in a preheated oven, 200°C (400°F), Gas Mark 6, for about 20 minutes until golden and the pastry is well risen. Transfer to a wire rack and leave to cool for 20 minutes. Serve warm or cold.

BARELY-DEAD-HUMAN ROLLS

It's imperative that the meat used for this dish is fresh,
so it isn't suitable for those who prefer their food in a state of rot or decay.

UNICORN PIES

Free-range unicorns have always been as rare as gold dust but they were worth seeking out for a special occasion. If the price was prohibitive, more patient individuals used to hang around a motorway at dusk, where they might be fortunate enough to spot some roadkill. When all else failed, hungry hunters who still wanted pie on the menu, would prepare this version, which is very close to the original.

Sufficient.—for 4 pies

1 tablespoon olive oil

8 boneless, skinless chicken thighs, about 625 g (1¼ lb), cubed

1 onion, chopped

2 garlic cloves, finely chopped

2 tablespoons plain flour

150 ml (¼ pint) white wine

200 ml (7 fl oz) chicken stock

few sprigs of, or a little dried, thyme

25 g (1 oz) butter, plus extra for greasing

125 g (4 oz) mushrooms, sliced

470 g (15 oz) shortcrust pastry

beaten egg, to glaze

Method.—Heat the oil in a large frying pan, add the chicken and fry, stirring, until beginning to colour. Add the onion and fry until the chicken is golden and the onion softened. Stir in the garlic and flour. Add the wine, stock and thyme and season with salt and pepper. Bring to the boil, stirring, then cover and simmer for 30 minutes until the chicken is cooked through. Heat the butter in a small frying pan and fry the mushrooms until golden. Add to the chicken and leave to cool.

Reserve one-third of the pastry, then cut the rest into 4 pieces. Roll out each piece, then use to line 4 greased individual springform tins, 10 cm (4 inches) in diameter and 4.5 cm (1 ¾ inches) deep. Roll out the reserved pastry and cut out lids.

Spoon the chicken filling into the pies, brush the top edges with beaten egg, then add the lids and press the pastry edges together. Bake on a baking sheet in a preheated oven, 190°C (375°C), Gas Mark 5, for 30 minutes until golden. Leave to stand for 5 minutes, then loosen the edges, transfer to a plate and remove the tins.

UNICORN PIES

Do not under any circumstances be tempted to use farm-reared unicorn for this dish.
The results will be simply unpalatable.

BAKED EYEBALLS WITH SNOT

If a Cyclops is invited to dinner, be sure to serve baked eyeballs as a starter or snack—sight begets sight and a mouthful of the delicately baked morsels will boost the vision of their solitary eye. However, they're not cheap so, if you can't source your own, you might be able to fob off your dinner guests with this cheap—but equally tasty—alternative.

Sufficient.—for 4 monster servings

8 large flat mushrooms, stalks trimmed
8 slices of Taleggio cheese
75 g (3 oz) dried breadcrumbs
1 garlic clove, crushed
6 tablespoons olive oil
bunch of basil leaves, finely chopped

25 g (1 oz) Parmesan cheese, finely
  grated
25 g (1 oz) toasted pine nuts, chopped,
  plus extra to serve
salt and pepper

Method.—Put the mushrooms on a baking sheet and top each one with a slice of Taleggio. Mix together the breadcrumbs and garlic and scatter a little over each mushroom. Drizzle with some of the olive oil and bake in a preheated oven, 200°C (400°F), Gas Mark 6, for 15–20 minutes until golden and crispy.

Meanwhile, mix together the basil, Parmesan, pine nuts and remaining oil and season to taste. Drizzle the pesto over the mushrooms and scatter over a few extra pine nuts to serve.

SLUG AND SLIME PIES

If a Mummy or a Swamp Creature invites you to supper, chances are you'll be treated to a mouth-watering Slug and Slime Pie. The pastry must be really thick to contain the oozing slime, and the best pies use fattened, farm-reared slugs. If you have a moral aversion to factory farming, let your hosts know in advance—they will probably prepare this slug-free FairFarm® version instead.

Sufficient.—for 8 pies

25 g (1 oz) butter
1 tablespoon olive oil
1 onion, finely chopped
250 g (8 oz) mixed mushrooms, sliced
2 garlic cloves, finely chopped
3 sprigs of thyme, leaves torn from stems, plus extra for sprinkling (optional)

500 g (1 lb) ready-made puff pastry, defrosted if frozen
a little flour, for dusting
120 ml (4 fl oz) full-fat crème fraîche
175 g (6 oz) Stilton cheese, diced with rind removed
beaten egg, to glaze
sea salt flakes

Method.—Heat the butter and oil in a frying pan, add the onion and fry for a few minutes until just beginning to soften, then add the mushrooms and garlic and fry, stirring, until golden. Remove from the heat, add the thyme leaves and leave to cool.

Roll out the pastry thinly on a lightly floured surface and trim to a 35 cm (14 inch) square, then cut into 16 squares. Spoon the mushroom mixture over the centre of 8 of the squares, then top with crème fraîche and Stilton. Brush the edges of the pastry with beaten egg, then cover each with a second pastry square.

Press the edges of the pastry together well and crimp the edges, if liked. Transfer to a baking sheet, then slash the tops with a knife, brush with more beaten egg and sprinkle with salt flakes and extra thyme, if liked.

Bake in a preheated oven, 200°C (400°F), Gas Mark 6, for 20 minutes until well risen and golden brown.

MASHED BOGEY TARTS

Fresh bogeys used to be a much-loved treat but they were also incredibly messy to eat. To solve the problem of spillages at underling parties, a stay-at-home Cyclops created a bogey tart 300 years ago. However, snot intolerance has become a big issue in recent times and many schools and party venues now ban it. This allergy-friendly version has been adopted in place of the original recipe.

Sufficient.—for 16 tarts

1 sheet of filo pastry, 48 x 23 cm (19 x 9 inches), defrosted if frozen

25 g (1 oz) butter, melted

1 ripe avocado

juice of 1 lime

½ mild red chilli, deseeded and finely chopped, plus extra to garnish (optional)

1 spring onion, finely chopped

2 tablespoons finely chopped coriander, plus extra to garnish (optional)

salt and pepper

Method.—Unfold the pastry sheet, brush with butter, then cut into 32 small squares, each about 5 cm (2 inches). Gently press 1 square into each of 16 sections of 2 x 12-hole mini muffin tins, then add a second square of pastry to each at right angles to the first for a petal-like effect.

Bake in a preheated oven, 190°C (375°F), Gas Mark 5, for 4–5 minutes until golden. Lift the filo cups out of the tins and transfer to a wire rack to cool.

Halve and stone the avocado, then scoop the flesh out of the shell and mash with the lime juice or blitz in a food processor. Add the chilli, spring onion and coriander, season lightly with salt and pepper and mix together.

Spoon the guacamole into the filo cups, garnish with extra chopped chilli and coriander, if liked, and serve within 1 hour of finishing as the avocado discolours.

MASHED BOGEY TARTS

Bogey intolerance is a growing concern, particularly among parents. It's now considered proper to warn your guests in advance should you prepare a bogey dish.

SMALL INTESTINE SKEWERS

These are perfect for family picnics. The traditional recipe has been altered somewhat: the skewers take on the flavour of whatever the human victim last ate and, as prey were often captured outside kebab shops late on Saturday evenings (an easy catch due to alcohol-induced stupor), the quality of intestines dropped dramatically and the original recipe went out of favour.

Sufficient.—for 10 skewers

6 tablespoons dark soy sauce
2 tablespoons sesame oil
1 teaspoon Chinese 5-spice powder
375 g (12 oz) boneless, skinless chicken
   breasts, cut into long, thin strips
cucumber, cut into strips, to serve

Sauce
4 tablespoons peanut butter
1 tablespoon dark soy sauce
½ teaspoon ground coriander
½ teaspoon ground cumin
pinch of paprika or chilli powder
8 tablespoons water

Method.—Place the soy sauce, sesame oil and 5-spice powder in a bowl and mix together. Add the chicken and toss together to coat in the marinade. Cover and leave to marinate in the refrigerator for 1 hour, stirring from time to time.

Thread the chicken, zigzag fashion, on to 10 soaked bamboo skewers (soaking them in warm water for 30 minutes will prevent the sticks burning while cooking), and place the chicken under a preheated hot grill for 8–10 minutes, turning once, until golden and cooked through.

Meanwhile, put all the sauce ingredients in a small saucepan and heat, stirring, until warm and well mixed. Transfer to a small serving bowl.

Place the bowl of sauce on a serving plate with the cucumber on one side and the hot chicken skewers around it.

SMALL INTESTINE SKEWERS

If you have humans in captivity, alter the flavour of this dish by force-feeding them a food of your choice. It can make for a great flavour-guessing dinner party game!

How to Carve a Human

Flesh-eaters are very discerning about their meat and different members of the community favour different human cuts, which is worth remembering when you're entertaining. A skilled human dismemberer will trim and carve the meat for you, so it is easier to prepare. Don't shy away from cheaper cuts—many are coming back into favour and, if properly cooked, these can be as tasty as prime joints. You should also embrace nose-to-tail-end eating by making use of every last ear and eyeball.

(I) BRAIN
A delicacy for Zombies—best eaten raw or simply fried in belly fat.

(II) EARS (EARWAX)
Ears need to be slow-cooked in order to be edible but larger specimens will yield a good crop of earwax, which is particularly prized by Ogres and Giant Apes as a cooking ingredient.

(III) EYEBALLS
Perfect for snacking, as well as adding to soups and stews.

(IV) NOSE
Giants sometimes add noses to the menu but most other diners will shy away from the chewy consistency of the cartilage. However, snot is a delicacy and you should try to extract every last drop—use a syringe if necessary.

(V) NECK
Vampires particularly enjoy this cut after bloodletting. It needs to be carefully separated from the vertebrae using a very sharp knife.

(VI) RIBS
Perfect for barbecues and dipping; also used as toothpicks by Giants and Ogres. Serve as a rack or individually, depending on the size and appetite of your guests.

(VII) BICEPS
The biceps of body builders are prized by part-mechanical monsters, while sloth-like Yetis prefer the leaner meat of bingo wings. Trim away the skin, as this can be tough.

(VIII) HEART AND LUNGS
Avoid fatty or disease-ridden organs and prepare fresh for optimum flavour.

(IX) TORSO
This can be served as a whole joint
or cut into chops.

(X) ENTRAILS
These should be served warm, direct
from the body—otherwise preserve in
vinegar and enjoy pickled when your
favourite humans are out of season.

(XI) FLANK
If the human has been exercising to
excess the flank can become tough
—source from couch potato shops to
ensure a flabby, fat-laden piece of meat.

(XII) RUMP
A well-rounded rump will provide a
filling meal for a houseful of guests,
although Giants will easily consume
an entire rump each. Allow to rest
before carving.

(XIII) TOENAILS
While fingers and toes are fiddly to
eat and yield little meat, nails are a
real treat. Try not to dislodge the dirt
underneath when you prise off the nails
—this adds to the flavour.

SCOTCH EGGS

These eggs were originally prepared with genuine Scottish people, with special care taken to remove all traces of tartan-ware and bagpipes before mincing—even the smallest amount could result in an uncontrollable desire to dance a jig. When genuine Scots were elusive, this tasty alternative was used instead.

Sufficient.—for 4 eggs

40 g (1½ oz) plain flour
2 teaspoons mustard powder
75 g (3 oz) fresh fine breadcrumbs
5 eggs, at room temperature
1 litre (1¾ pints) groundnut oil,
    rapeseed oil or sunflower oil

2 heaped tablespoons finely
    chopped chives
350 g (11½ oz) sausagemeat

To serve
black pepper

Method.—Mix together the flour and mustard powder in a wide shallow bowl, place the breadcrumbs in another bowl and beat 1 of the eggs in a third bowl.

Boil the remaining eggs in a medium saucepan (3½ minutes for soft yolks, 6 minutes for firmer yolks or 8 minutes for hard-boiled). Remove, place in a bowl of cold water and set aside for 5 minutes. When cool, shell the eggs and set aside.

Heat the oil in a deep-fryer or a large, deep-sided, heavy-based saucepan (so it comes no more than halfway up the sides) over a medium heat to 180°C (350°F) or until a cube of bread browns in 30 seconds.

Meanwhile, mix the chives into the sausagemeat with a fork. Divide the mixture into 4, then shape each piece into a round patty. Place 1 egg in the centre of each patty and gently encase the eggs in the sausagemeat. Roll each in the seasoned flour, then in the beaten egg and finally in the breadcrumbs until completely coated.

Deep-fry the eggs for 5–7 minutes or until deep golden brown and the sausagemeat is cooked through. Remove and drain on kitchen paper. Serve cut in half with freshly ground black pepper.

Note: this recipe has been translated for use by Mummies

BELOVED-FAMILY-PET PIE

The age-old adversary of every Under-the-Bed and In-the-Cupboard Monster, this pie was a great way to make use of over-inquisitive moggies and mongrels that came sniffing around during a scaring or raid. The more loved the pet the better it tasted, so scarers didn't bother collecting unwanted Christmas puppies or neglected hamsters. Many tribes now suffer with cat dander allergy, so they prepare this version instead.

Sufficient.—for 6–8 monster servings of pie

500 g (1 lb) sausagemeat

500 g (1 lb) boneless, skinless chicken
   thighs, chopped

125 g (4 oz) smoked bacon, diced

5 cloves, roughly crushed

¼ teaspoon ground allspice

small bunch of sage

1 Braeburn apple, cored and sliced

1 egg yolk mixed with 1 tablespoon water

salt and pepper

Hot-water crust pastry

175 g (6 oz) lard

175 ml (6 fl oz) milk and water,
   mixed half and half

2 teaspoons English mustard

375 g (12 oz) plain flour

¼ teaspoon salt

Method.—Make the pastry. Put the lard, milk and water in a saucepan. Heat gently until the lard has just melted. Stir in the mustard. Bring just to the boil, then tip into a bowl containing the flour and salt. Mix with a wooden spoon until it forms a smooth soft ball. Cover the bowl and leave for 10 minutes until cool enough to handle.

Meanwhile, mix together the sausagemeat, chicken, bacon, cloves, allspice and plenty of salt and pepper in a bowl.

Knead the pastry lightly, then reserve one-third. Press the remaining warm pastry over the base and sides of a deep 18 cm (7 inch) loose-bottomed cake tin. Spoon in half the meat filling and level. Cover with half the sage leaves, then the apple slices, then spoon over the rest of the filling. Level and top with the remaining sage. Brush the edges of the pastry with the egg glaze.

Roll a lid out of the reserved pastry, arrange on the pie and press the edges together. Trim off the excess and use it to decorate. Make a slit in the top of the pie, then brush with the egg glaze. Bake in a preheated oven, 180°C (350°F), Gas Mark 4, for 1½ hours, covering with foil after 40 minutes, when golden. Leave to cool then refrigerate for 3–4 hours or overnight. Remove from the tin and cut into 6–8 wedges to serve.

DRAGON'S EGG TARTS

Larger than an average egg and with added health and healing powers, these tarts used to fly out of monster markets when they were in season. Cliff and cave dwellers were often able to harvest their own dragon eggs but human raiders or anyone with vertigo had to rely on a good mating season for an abundant supply. To avoid disappointment, this mock egg version of the recipe was introduced to great response.

Sufficient.—for 4 tarts

470 g (15 oz) shortcrust pastry, cut into
    4 pieces
1 tablespoon olive oil
1 onion, chopped
1 red pepper, cored, deseeded and diced
75 g (3 oz) ready-diced chorizo sausage
2 garlic cloves, finely chopped

¼ teaspoon smoked paprika
2 bay leaves
200 g (7 oz) can chopped tomatoes
150 g (5 oz) cherry tomatoes, halved
4 eggs
salt and pepper

Method.— Roll out each piece of pastry on a lightly floured surface until a little larger than a greased 12 cm (5 inch) fluted loose-bottomed tart tin. Lift the pastry into the tins, then press over the base and sides. Trim off the excess so that it stands a little above the top of the tins. Prick the bases with a fork and chill for 15 minutes.

Heat the oil in a saucepan and fry the onion, red pepper and chorizo for 5 minutes until softened. Stir in the garlic, paprika, bay leaves and canned tomatoes and season. Simmer gently, uncovered, for 15 minutes, stirring from time to time until thickened.

Meanwhile, line the tarts with nonstick baking paper, add baking beans and place on a baking sheet. Bake in a preheated oven, 190°C (375°F), Gas Mark 5, for 8 minutes. Remove the paper and beans and bake for a further 4 minutes until golden.

Stir the cherry tomatoes into the sauce. Discard the bay leaves and spoon the sauce into the pastry cases. Make a dip in the centre, break an egg into each and bake for 5–8 minutes. Remove from the tins and serve warm.

BLOOD, BONES AND BITS TART

Sticklers for leftovers would always keep the original tart recipe close to hand. Confident cooks would adjust the ingredients and quantities to suit their pantry. However, those who were afflicted with fussy offspring got fed up with scraping good tart into the refuse and, rather than let them go hungry, new-age monsters pandered to their faddiness by preparing this beanstalk-hugging, human-friendly alternative.

Sufficient.—for 6 monster servings of tart

470 g (15 oz) shortcrust pastry
1 tablespoon olive oil
1 onion, chopped
200 g (7 oz) raw, trimmed beetroot,
    coarsely grated
4 eggs
250 ml (8 fl oz) milk

1 teaspoon Dijon mustard
small bunch of thyme, leaves torn
    from stems
150 g (5 oz) goats' cheese log, cut into
    6 thick slices
salt and cayenne pepper

Method.—Roll out the pastry on a lightly floured surface until a little larger than a greased 24 cm (9½ inch) fluted loose-bottomed tart tin. Lift the pastry over a rolling pin, drape into the tin, then press over the base and sides. Trim off the excess pastry with scissors so that it stands a little above the top of the tin. Chill for 15 minutes.

Meanwhile, heat the oil in a frying pan, add the onion and fry until softened. Add the beetroot and cook for 2–3 minutes. Beat the eggs, milk and mustard together in a bowl. Add the onions, some of the thyme leaves and a generous amount of salt and cayenne pepper. Leave to stand for 5 minutes.

Put the tart case on a baking sheet and pour the beetroot mix into the tart case. Arrange the cheese slices in a ring on top of the tart and sprinkle with the remaining thyme leaves and a little salt and cayenne pepper.

Bake in a preheated oven, 180°C (350°F), Gas Mark 4, for 40–45 minutes until the filling is set. Leave to cool for 15 minutes, remove the tin and transfer to a plate to serve.

CORPSE QUICHES

For reasons unknown, humans called Lorraine apparently make the tastiest quiches. However, in recent years, this particular name seems to have waned in popularity and Lorraines are now few and far between—those that do exist tend to be older and chewier. These Lorraine-free quiches will still be a talking point at your shindig.

Sufficient.—for 6 quiches

325 g (11 oz) gluten-free pastry
rice flour, for dusting
1 tablespoon sunflower oil
4 smoked streaky bacon rashers,
    about 75 g (3 oz), diced
1 small onion, chopped

125 g (4 oz) Cheddar cheese, grated
3 eggs
200 ml (7 fl oz) milk
1 teaspoon mustard powder
1 tablespoon chopped chives
salt and pepper

Method.— Cut the pastry into 6 pieces, then roll out 1 piece between 2 sheets of clingfilm until a little larger than a greased individual 10 cm (4 inch) fluted loose-bottomed tart tin. Remove the top sheet of clingfilm, turn the pastry over, drape into the tart tin and remove the top sheet of clingfilm. Press the pastry into the base and sides of the tin with fingers dusted in rice flour. Trim off the excess pastry with scissors a little above the top of the tin. Patch any cracks or breaks with pastry trimmings. Repeat to make 6 tarts. Put on a baking sheet and chill for 15 minutes.

Meanwhile, heat the oil in a frying pan, add the bacon and onion and fry for 5 minutes, stirring until golden.

Divide three-quarters of the cheese between the tart cases. Sprinkle the onion and bacon mix on top. Beat the eggs, milk and mustard in a jug with a little salt and pepper, then pour into the tarts. Sprinkle with the chives and the remaining cheese.

Bake in a preheated oven, 190°C (375°F), Gas Mark 5, for 25–30 minutes until the tops are golden and the pastry bases cooked through. Leave to cool for 5 minutes, then remove from the tins and serve.

CORPSE QUICHES

Vampires will prefer a fresh cadaver to be used for this dish.
Giant spiders will prefer the dried variety.

SWEET GOOEY BAKED BRAIN

Slow-baked and gooey, this was the perfect way to end a meal in the pre-organic era. Cooks needed to gauge the quantities based on their guests—one brain between two for smaller monsters, or around ten brains per Giant. With organic brains being harder to procure, the original dish decreased in popularity and this version took its place. It doesn't have the wow factor of baked brain but a couple of Crispy Baked Rib Bones (*see* page 112) for dipping will help to elevate the dish.

Sufficient.—for 4 monsters to share

300 g (10 oz) whole baby Brie or
    Camembert (in a wooden box)
25 g (1 oz) pecan nuts
3 tablespoons maple syrup
3 tablespoons soft brown sugar
sprigs of thyme, leaves torn from stems

Method.—Remove any plastic packaging from the cheese and return it to its wooden box. Place on a baking sheet and bake in a preheated oven, 200°C (400°F), Gas Mark 6, for 15 minutes.

Meanwhile, toast the pecans in a small frying pan for 3–5 minutes until lightly browned, then set aside. Put the maple syrup and sugar in a small saucepan and bring to the boil. Cook for 1 minute until foamy.

Remove the cheese from the oven and cut a small cross in the centre. Drizzle over the maple syrup, scatter with the pecans and thyme and serve with plenty of crusty bread.

SWEET GOOEY BAKED BRAIN

If serving Giants you will, as always, need to multiply the portions by at least 10.

SHRIMP SKEWERS

Short humans were traditionally hunted by monster offspring in training camps, as they were easier to catch. They also packed a real flavour punch so were prized for the cooking pot once caught. Humans over 5 feet in height were traditionally used in pies and tarts—the original recipe for these skewers called for prime cuts of diminutive people. When fishing became a more popular pastime than human hunting for certain tribes, this pescatarian variation of the original recipe was introduced.

Sufficient.—for 4 skewers

5 lemon grass stalks
4 tablespoons sweet chilli sauce, plus
   extra to serve
2 tablespoons chopped coriander
2 tablespoons sesame oil
20 raw tiger prawns, peeled but tails left on

Method.—Take 1 of the lemon grass stalks and remove the outer leaves. Finely slice it and place it in a bowl along with the sweet chilli sauce, coriander and oil. Place the prawns in the marinade, cover and leave to marinate in the refrigerator for 1 hour or overnight.

Remove the prawns from the marinade. Take the remaining 4 lemon grass stalks and remove a few of the outer layers to give you a thin lemon grass skewer. Make a hole through each prawn at its thickest part using a metal skewer, then thread 5 of the prawns on to a lemon grass stalk. Repeat with the remaining lemon grass and prawns.

Place the prawn skewers on a barbecue and cook for 4 minutes on each side or until the prawns have turned pink and are firm to the touch.

Serve the prawns straight from the barbecue with sweet chilli sauce or Intestine Sauce (*see* page 113) for dipping.

FLAYED MINION

The most miserable minions offered up the choicest cuts for the original dish, so they were worked hard for good muscle growth. Unfortunately, this also meant feeding them well, which is why this wasn't an everyday meal. Many communities also chose to keep their captured humans for prolonged servitude—or became fond of them over the years and treated them more like pets than workers—so animal flesh became standard in this recipe, as below.

Sufficient.—for 4

50 g (2 oz) butter
4 shallots, finely chopped
1 tablespoon wholegrain mustard
1 teaspoon Dijon mustard
2 tablespoons ready-made
    black olive tapenade
150 ml (¼ pint) cider

4 thick fillet steaks, about
    200 g (7 oz) each
2 tablespoons coarsely ground
    black peppercorns
2 tablespoons crème fraîche
2 tablespoons chopped tarragon
salt and pepper

Method.—Heat the butter in a frying pan until it has melted and is beginning to froth. Add the shallots and fry gently for 5–6 minutes until softened. Add the wholegrain and Dijon mustards and the tapenade and pour in the cider. Simmer gently for 2 minutes, then remove from the heat.

Press the fillet steaks into the black pepper. Cook on a hot barbecue for 3–4 minutes on each side or until cooked to your liking. Rest on warm serving plates while finishing off the sauce.

Stir the crème fraîche and tarragon into the tapenade sauce, season to taste with salt and pepper and gently warm the sauce without letting it boil. Pour a little of the sauce over each fillet steak and serve immediately. Try with steamed asparagus, homemade chips and a dish of mustardy mayonnaise.

Cave Games

Every good party should include a selection of parlour games. Many members of the community have short attention spans so will need entertaining once the dinner plates are cleared away. It's important to choose games based on your guests—avoid anything fast-moving for Zombies, and dressing-up games are considered inappropriate for Mummies. Likewise, hiding games and Trolls aren't a good match, as they're liable to go into premature hibernation if they remain undiscovered for more than ten minutes.

PIN THE HEART ON THE HUMAN

Draw the outline of a life-sized human on paper. Give one of your guests a human heart to hold, with a pin through its middle. Blindfold your guest, and spin them around a few times. Then ask them to pin the heart on the human. If you have any actual humans dining with you, make it clear to other guests that they're only supposed to pin the heart on the drawing, not on the real humans.

SPIN THE THIGHBONE

Any bone will do but Giants and clawed individuals will find it easier to play with a large bone. When the bone points towards a guest, they must perform a party piece— this could be their specialist skill (howling, fire-breathing, chest-beating etc.) or a short piano or poetry recital.

ADAM'S APPLE BOBBING

This game makes a real mess so use an old bathtub or wheelbarrow to hold the water and place a plastic sheet underneath. Adam's apples should be purchased from a reputable supplier, or your guests might end up bobbing with a collection of unlanced boils or growths of dubious origin.

PASS THE POTION

This is a great way to use up leftover potions and unwanted Christmas grog. Pass the potion bottle around the assembled group and play some music—when the music stops, whoever is holding the potion must drink it. Be warned, this is a game for serious partygoers.

SNAP

When you suggest a game of snap, human guests will be waiting for you to produce a pack of cards but the monster community will be expecting a pile of bones. The aim of the game is to see who can snap the most bones within a set time frame—usually the time it takes a Zombie to say his or her name.

HIDE AND SHRIEK

This is best played if you've invited Under-the-Bed Monsters to your party, as their scaring abilities are second to none. Ask everyone else to go and hide, then the seeker has to try and petrify as many players as possible.

Hoxton Street Monster Supplies

ESTᴰ 1818

~ Purveyor of Quality Goods for Monsters of Every Kind ~

JAMS AND PRESERVES

INCLUDING

THICKEST HUMAN SNOT
& CHUNKY ORGAN CHUTNEY

GALLSTONE AND BILE SMOOTHIE

If you're a firm follower of the monster raw juice trend, add this recipe to your repertoire. It traditionally contained gallstones for an energy burst, while the bile added a deliciously sour aftertaste. It was often drunk as a breakfast-on-the-go or a midnight snack before human baiting. However, many health-conscious communities found that bile sat rather heavily on the stomach, which led to juice guru Dr Jekyll creating this lighter alternative.

Sufficient.—for 4 smoothies

3 tablespoons crème de cassis or spiced
   red fruit cordial
250 g (8 oz) mixed frozen berries
500 g (1 lb) fat-free fromage frais
400 ml (14 fl oz) milk
1 vanilla pod, split in half lengthways
toasted flaked almonds, to decorate

Method.—Put the crème de cassis or cordial in a saucepan over a low heat and gently heat, then add the berries. Stir, cover and cook for about 5 minutes or until the fruit has thawed and is beginning to collapse. Remove from the heat and cool completely.

Process most of the berry mixture with the fromage frais and milk in a food processor or blender until smooth.

Scrape in the seeds from the vanilla pod and beat to combine.

Fold the reserved berries into the fromage frais mixture until just combined. Spoon into 4 glasses and serve immediately, decorated with toasted almonds.

HELL BROTH

If you can't shift that winter cold, a flagon of this fiery potion will clear your nostrils and flush the phlegm away in an instant. Brewed in the deepest depths of hell by indentured humans and banished monsters (fangless Vampires, cuddly Giants, water-breathing Dragons, operatic Werewolves etc.) the agony of eternal damnation is apparent in every sip.

Sufficient.—for 350 ml (12 fl oz)

1 lemon
2 cm (¾ inch) piece of fresh root ginger
1 garlic clove
1 apple, about 100 g (3½ oz)
1 carrot, about 150 g (5 oz)
2 celery sticks
100 g (3½ oz) alfalfa sprouts

Method.—Roughly peel the lemon, ginger and garlic. Juice all the ingredients together.

Pour the juice into a glass and serve immediately.

VERY BLOODY MARY

A classic Vampire mocktail—this was often served at celebratory after-bite parties. The taste varied considerably depending on the vintage and calibre of human blood, so this modern version was created to ensure consistency of flavour, and as a stand-in when hunting packs came back empty-handed. It should always be prepared fresh.

Sufficient.—for 4 Very Bloody Marys

2 garlic cloves, chopped

2 celery sticks, chopped, plus extra
with leafy tops to serve

1 tablespoon chopped onion

500 g (1 lb) ripe tomatoes

300 ml (½ pint) tomato juice

juice of 2 limes

1 teaspoon celery salt

2–3 tablespoons Worcestershire sauce

125 ml (4 fl oz) vodka (optional)

Tabasco sauce, to taste

lime wedges, to serve

Method.—Put all the ingredients, except the vodka and Tabasco sauce, in a food processor or blender and whizz until smooth. Press the mixture through a fine sieve.

Add the vodka, if using, and Tabasco sauce to taste and pour into 4 glasses. Serve with leafy sprigs of celery and lime wedges.

VERY BLOODY MARY

If at all possible, try to find blood from humans called Mary.
You won't regret the extra effort.

UNFILTERED SWAMP CIDER

Swamp dwellers can freely indulge in this natural tonic by dipping a cup into the murky depths and taking a swig. The probiotic craze has led to a number of savvy Swamp Creatures bottling their cider and selling it at local organic fairs. The price rises exponentially with the smell and foul taste, and health-food junkies are prepared to pay a premium for samples bubbling away with natural noxious gases.

Sufficient.—for 300 ml (½ pint)

1 fennel bulb, about 150 g (5 oz)
1 apple, about 100 g (3½ oz)
1 carrot, about 150 g (5 oz)
grated nutmeg, to sprinkle

Method.—Juice all the ingredients together.
Pour the juice into a glass and sprinkle with a large pinch of nutmeg. Serve immediately.

ZOMBIE LEMONADE

It can be difficult for the undead to keep up appearances and this brightly coloured cocktail was created to give Zombies an unearthly green glow. It has since been discovered by teenage partygoers from other tribes, keen to impress their buddies by glowing in the dark. Naturally, Under-the-Bed and In-the-Cupboard Monsters should avoid it on nocturnal scaring missions.

Sufficient.—for 500 ml (17 fl oz)

2 lemons, plus extra to decorate
30 g (1¼ oz) spinach
1 cucumber, about 350 g (11½ oz)
sparkling water

Method.—Juice the lemons with the spinach and cucumber.
Pour the juice into a glass, top up with sparkling water and decorate with a wedge of lemon.

SATANIC SMOOTHIE

A quick fix for those seeking revenge or retribution—this concoction can carry a curse that will see the drinker banished to the underworld at Satan's leisure. You can increase the curse for even greater suffering but this will affect the taste so could arouse suspicion. If you don't add the curse, it makes a very pleasant aperitif at dinner parties and cocktail evenings.

Sufficient.—for 250 ml (8 fl oz)

1 lemon
2 pomegranates, about 500 g (1 lb) in total
200 g (7 oz) blueberries

Method.—Roughly peel the lemon. Remove the seeds from the pomegranate by cutting the fruit in half, then holding the halved fruit over a bowl and hitting the skin with a wooden spoon so that the seeds fall into the bowl.

Juice all the ingredients together.

Pour the juice into a glass and serve immediately.

SATANIC SMOOTHIE

CAUTION

Be sure to keep cursed and non-cursed smoothies separate.
Nothing upsets the smooth running of a soirée quite like
a guest being accidentally banished to the pits of hell.

Festivals & Special Occasions

There are a number of important festivals throughout the year—from full moon parties and dragon coming-of-fire rituals, to Day of the Undead and Mummies' Day. We've put together some top tips to help make your special occasion even more special. Whether it's choice consumables, decorative flourishes or ideas to improve personal hygiene, these can be adapted by every community for every celebration.

ANNIVERSARY

Woe betide any errant husband that forgets an important anniversary. Show your other half you care on your 500th or 1,000th wedding anniversary by presenting them with a bunch of dead roses. If you put them in a vase of swamp water they will slowly decompose and the putrid smell will permeate around your cave, coffin or lair.

MUMMIES' DAY

Mummies love being singled out on their special day—make it even more special by clubbing together for a new set of bandages or preparing some 1,000-Year Curse-Reverse Cookies (*see* page 45) to try and remove the curtain of evil that hangs over them.

DAY OF THE UNDEAD

If you've been invited to a party by Vampires, Vampire Bats, Zombies, Mummies, Werewolves or other undead friends, it is customary not to talk about the living world. Instead, stick to topics such as shape shifting, blood gorging and the upcoming elections for the local Necromancer.

CHRISTMAS

Many members of the community only began to celebrate this human festival at the beginning of the last century but it is now an important day in the calendar. It is traditional to prepare a whole roasted side of human—either ask your local dismemberer to cut and trim it for you, or refer to our guide on page 124.

VALENTINE'S DAY

The older generation eschewed romance for a swift knock on the head with a club. But if you are wooing a Werewolf, dating a Dragon or courting a Cyclops, this is the day to make your intentions known—send a card with a simple love note or poem:

Corpses are dead
Adipose tissue
Entrails are rancid,
And so are you.

HALLOWEEN

This strange human celebration of all things dead and undead offers the ideal hunting opportunity, as members of the community can freely mingle with their human prey. If you have a sweet tooth you can also steal the sweets that small people collect from their neighbours—perfect as a starter before a meal of angst-ridden teenager.

Index

TUCKED RIGHT BEHIND HOXTON STREET MONSTER SUPPLIES IN LONDON YOU WILL FIND THE MINISTRY OF STORIES, A WRITING AND MENTORING CENTRE WHERE CHILDREN AND YOUNG PEOPLE CAN COME AND DISCOVER THEIR OWN GIFT FOR WRITING.

Through a range of innovative writing programmes, and one-to-one mentoring, we help young people discover and realise their own creative potential. We build confidence, self-respect and communication skills in both workshops for schools and out-of-school writing clubs.

Then we provide a publishing platform for young writers, so these fresh, exciting voices are shared with the world.

By making writing fun and accessible we help young people find their voices. We challenge their expectations, build their aspirations, and nurture their development, skills and imaginations.

The Ministry of Stories is a charity. We rely on donations from companies, trusts and lovely people like you to continue the work we do. Thank you for supporting us by buying this book. Go to ministryofstories.org to learn more about how you could support us.

Registered Charity No. 1138553 | Limited Company No. 07317370

An Hachette UK Company
www.hachette.co.uk

First published in Great Britain in 2016
by Mitchell Beazley, a division of
Octopus Publishing Group Ltd
Carmelite House
50 Victoria Embankment
London EC4Y 0DZ
www.octopusbooks.co.uk

Recipe Title Copyright
© Hoxton Street Monster Supplies Limited 2016
Text Copyright
© Octopus Publishing Group Limited 2016

ISBN 978-1-78472-230-2

A CIP catalogue record for this book
is available from the British Library.

Printed and bound in China

10 9 8 7 6 5 4 3 2 1

Commissioning Editor: Joe Cottington
Editor: Pollyanna Poulter
Creative Director: Jonathan Christie
Designer: Alistair Hall at We Made This
Production Controller: Sarah Kramer
Illustrator: Caroline Church
Additional text: Cara Frost-Sharratt

Standard level spoon measurements are used
in all recipes.

1 tablespoon = one 15 ml spoon
1 teaspoon = one 5 ml spoon

Both imperial and metric measurements have been
given in all recipes. Use one set of measurements
only and not a mixture of both.

Ovens should be preheated to the specific
temperature—if using a fan-assisted oven, follow
manufacturer's instructions for adjusting the time
and the temperature.

All eggs are medium, unless stated otherwise.

This book includes dishes made with nuts and nut
derivatives. It is advisable for customers with known
allergic reactions to nuts and nut derivatives and
those who may be potentially vulnerable to these
allergies, such as pregnant and nursing mothers,
invalids, the elderly, babies and children, to avoid
dishes made with nuts and nut oils. It is also prudent
to check the labels of pre-prepared ingredients for
the possible inclusion of nut derivatives.

To test if a jam has reached setting point, drop
2 teaspoons of the jam on to a chilled saucer. Leave
to cool for a minute or two, then push the jam with
your finger. If the top wrinkles, the jam is ready.
Alternatively, if using a sugar thermometer, the jam
should reach 105°C (221°F).

To sterilize jars, wash the jars, then rinse well with
hot water, drain and stand in a roasting tin. Warm
in a preheated oven, 160°C (325°F), Gas Mark 3,
for 10 minutes. Alternatively, wash them in a
dishwasher and use as soon as the programme has
finished while still warm, but dry.

EST. ROTHERHAM 1148

GRIMM & C<u>o</u>

APOTHECARY

SUPPLIERS OF EVIL PLOTS, WILD SCHEMES & KITCHENWARE
— SINCE 1148 —

BUY THINGS:

APPROVED BY:

APOTHECARY
TO THE MAGICAL
2 DONCASTER GATE,
ROTHERHAM S65 1DJ
GRIMMANDCO.CO.UK

GRIMM & C<u>o</u>

GOOD 'EALTH. GRAHAM GRIMM.

THIRTEEN PRIZE MEDALS.

SPECIAL APPOINTMENT TO
H.R.H. PRINCE VLAD III (THE IMPALER) & THE ROYAL COURTS OF BELGIUM & ITALY.

HOXTON STREET
MONSTER SUPPLIES
LONDON

THE COLLYWOBBLES

HOXTON STREET MONSTER SUPPLIES'

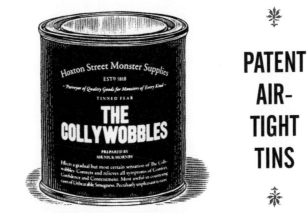

PATENT AIR-TIGHT TINS

FROM OUR ORIGINAL TINNED FEAR RANGE

Effects a gradual but most certain sensation of the Collywobbles. Corrects and relieves all symptoms of Comfort, Confidence and Contentment. Most useful in countering cases of Unbearable Smugness. Peculiarly unpleasant to taste, not suitable for those with heart conditions.

SOMBRE HARD-WEARING MONOCHROME TIN